To Brenda,
Thanks Again!

Secrets *THOSE* Credit Doctors Don't Want *YOU* to Know

~~~~~~
~~~~~~

CREDIT SECRET COURSE CERTIFICATE

To reward you for taking the first step towards improving your credit score by purchasing - *SECRETS THOSE CREDIT DOCTORS DON'T WANT YOU TO KNOW*, John Lee and Secrets of a Deal'ionaire Training is offering you and one guest an exclusive scholarship to attend the LIVE Credit Secret Intensive Seminar. At this world-famous program, you can transform your blueprint of credit scores and change the way you improve your credit forever.

To redeem your scholarship and register visit www.theDealionaire.com *

Use Reference #_____when you register.

(If you were not given a reference #, use your book receipt # or promotion code)

Secrets of a Deal'ionaire Training

~~~~~~
~~~~~~

* This offer is open to all purchasers of *SECRETS THOSE CREDIT DOCTORS DON'T WANT YOU TO KNOW* by John Lee. Scholarship may only be applied to the Credit Secret Intensive Seminar and registration is subject to availability and/or changes to program schedule. This is a strictly limited time offer and the scholarship must be redeemed by the date shown on the website www.theDealionaire.com. The value of this scholarship is up to $500, as of March 2020. Additional fees and tuitions may apply at the time of registration. Registrants are responsible for travel, food and accommodations, if required and are under no additional financial obligation whatsoever to Secrets of a Dealionaire Training or John Lee. Secrets of a Deal'ionaire Training reserves the right to refuse admission, and to remove from the premises anyone it believes is disrupting the seminar.

Books by John Lee

Secrets of a Deal'ionaire – Creating Wealth One Small Deal at a Time (2014)

Landlord Pennies to Banker Dollars (2019)

Secrets Those Credit Doctors Don't Want You to Know – Book and Workbook (2015)

4 Simple Steps to Prevent ID Theft and IRS Tax Refund Theft (2015)

How to Improve Your Credit Score – What Everyone Needs to Know (2010)

Secrets *THOSE* Credit Doctors Don't Want *YOU* to Know

7 Simple Steps to a Higher Credit Score
&
Avoiding a Debt Sentence

Secrets *THOSE* Credit Doctors Don't Want *YOU* to Know

7 SIMPLE STEPS TO A HIGHER CREDIT SCORE & AVOIDING A DEBT SENTENCE

By

John Lee

Secrets *THOSE* Credit Doctors Don't Want *YOU* to Know

7 SIMPLE STEPS TO A HIGHER CREDIT SCORE
&
AVOIDING A DEBT SENTENCE

Acknowledgement and Dedication

This book came out of all of the misinformation being promoted today by all of *Those Credit Doctors*. I couldn't be quiet any longer after hearing all of the false guarantees I know not to be true.

Some acknowledgements definitely need to be mentioned. I could not have shared this information without a little help from my friends (well, maybe a lot of help from my friends).

First and Foremost, my wife Laura has done a spectacular job in putting this book together and making sense out of it. She has such a great way of making me look good. I am so fortunate to have been blessed with her. I will never be the same.

Second, I want to thank all of *Those Credit Doctors* that cause so much confusion and attempt to keep everything shrouded in mystery. Many choose to misinform instead of educating those of us that need it. That's why I was forced to come forward and write this.

The truth is the truth. I've worked with many that are credit impaired and most just need a little guidance. Education is so important in the credit world. It's not magic. Some of the guarantees *Those Credit Doctors* throw out there are amazingly unbelievable. Another reason *why* we put this together.

Next I want to acknowledge some of my good friends and mentors. I have had the privilege of working with and training with some of the best people on the planet.

My very good friend and mentor AJ Rassamni is my best friend and such an inspiration to me. He is a world-class business expert, inventor, author, trainer and speaker. If you ever get an opportunity to study and learn from AJ, you should.

There are so many that have helped me along my journey, and I would like to thank each one personally. The only thing stopping me is time and the number of pages I am allowed here.

Thank you to all of my great mentors and teachers that I am forever indebted to. You are all so much appreciated. If I can pass on half of what I have been taught the world will improve.

These pages are all dedicated to those who are improving their credit scores with education and not with *Those Credit Doctors* who don't want *You* to know this.

John Lee

Table of Contents:

Secrets *THOSE* Credit Doctors Don't Want *YOU* to Know

INTRODUCTION

Most of the information contained in this text has come from experience, i.e. blood, sweat, tears, trials and errors. What started off as a necessity from my own circumstances, turned into a lifetime quest to help others obtain financial intelligence in regard to their credit.

There seems to be a lack of good information when it comes to your financial and credit well- being. It is my intent to provide you with good information that you will be able to apply to your own situation and betterment. Just by opening these pages you are taking a very important and giant step towards upgrading your life.

Regardless of where you are currently there is always room for improvement. Our intent is that our experiences will be beneficial for you. Thank you for taking the time to increase your education and understanding of *Secrets THOSE Credit Doctors Don't Want YOU to Know.*

Secrets *THOSE* Credit Doctors Don't Want *YOU* to Know

7 SIMPLE STEPS TO A HIGHER CREDIT SCORE
&
AVOIDING A DEBT SENTENCE

Secrets *THOSE* Credit Doctors Don't Want *YOU* to Know

7 SIMPLE STEPS TO A HIGHER CREDIT SCORE
&
AVOIDING A DEBT SENTENCE

Chapter 1: Who Cares?

Chapter 1

Who Cares?

Why Should You Care?

"My friend…care for your psyche…know thyself, for once we know ourselves, we may learn how to care for ourselves."
~Socrates~

Why should *YOU* care about *YOUR* Credit Scores and having a good one? Many people don't care. Smart people do care. A good credit score will allow you to choose who you want to do business with instead of who will do business with you.

With a good credit score you will get much more favorable interest rates on your loan, e.g. mortgages, auto loans, credit cards and more.

You'll also get better rates on your insurance premiums, auto, homeowners and renters' insurance just to name a few. Many employers also check your credit before hiring you for employment.

What is a Credit Score?

According to Wikipedia a *credit score* is a numerical expression based on a level analysis of a person's credit files, to represent the creditworthiness of that person. A credit score is primarily based on credit report information typically sourced from credit bureaus.

Lenders, such as banks and credit card companies, use credit scores to evaluate the potential risk posed by lending money to consumers and to mitigate losses due to bad debt.

Lenders use credit scores to determine who qualifies for a loan, at what interest rate, and what credit limits. Lenders also use credit scores to determine which customers are likely to bring in the most revenue.

The use of credit or identity scoring prior to authorizing access or granting credit is an implementation of a trusted system. Credit scoring is not limited to banks.

Other organizations, such as mobile phone companies,   insurance companies, landlords, and government departments employ the same techniques.

Credit scoring also has much overlap with data mining, which uses many similar techniques. These techniques combine thousands of factors but are similar or identical.

Credit Score Ranges

Credit scores range between about 300 and 900 for mortgages. They are a little different for the auto industry and a little different still for other industries. They can all be improved upon.

Where Do You Start?

The first step in determining how to improve your credit score is to start where you are at right now. How do you do this? Let's begin by going over some basic facts as to how the credit bureaus come up with the scores in the first place.

Where Are You in Regard to Everyone Else?

How do you rank in credit scores with the rest of Americans? In the United States the average credit score across the country is 720. Which means half the people had a score greater than 720 and half of the people had a score below 720. With nearly three hundred million residents that is quite a range.

What if you have no credit score or a credit score of "Zero"?

In order to even get a credit score, you need these three things:

1) You must have a trade line at least six months old.

2) You must have at least one trade line updated at the bureau within the last six months.

3) The Social Security number you are using cannot be associated with the terrorist list or a dead person.

Just about everything cost less with a good credit score!

As you improve your scores, you will pay less when you buy on credit – whether you're purchasing a home, cell phone, automobile or signing up for credit cards.

The difference in interest rates can be tremendous.

The Difference in Interest for a Mortgage Can Be Substantial

Take for Example a 30-year mortgage:

$150,000 @ 7% - 360 months = **$997.95**/month

Total = **$359,263.35**

$150,000 @ 4% - 360 months = **$716.12**/month

Total = **$257,804.26**

Difference = **$281.83**/month

Total Savings = $101,459.09

Who Cares?

Just about everyone cares in one way or another in just about every industry from banks, finance companies, insurance companies and employers. One of the best reasons I know of for having a good credit score is all of the choices you have.

You have many more opportunities that those with a lower score do not have. *You* may *choose* who *you want* to do business with. Any way you look at it you are the winner and *You* are ultimately the one *Who Cares.*

Ok, so what's a *FICO* Score?

Chapter 2: What is a *FICO*?

Chapter 2

What is a FICO?

"Whatever *You* are, Be a Good One."
~Abraham Lincoln~

What are FICO scores?

What is your **FICO** score anyway? Actually, your *FICO* score is only one of three credit scores you have. There are three credit bureaus and they each have a separate score.

One of the three bureaus is *Experian*, which gives you the *FICO* score.

There is also *TransUnion* who assigns you an *Empirica* score.

The third bureau is *Equifax* who gives you a *Beacon* score.

Why they each have a different name and where it came from is beyond the scope of how to improve your score. Let's just say they are similar in the way that they rate your credit.

The scores can be dramatically different at each bureau due to the fact of different information being reported to different agencies and also at different times to the agencies. Some creditors report to all three bureaus while other creditors may report to only one or two of the reporting bureaus. That is why the scores can range so much between the bureaus.

It is important to know what all three of the bureaus are reporting about you. Your scores can be as much as dozens and even hundreds of points different between the three agencies.

How do they come up with the scores?

In order to improve your credit score, you need to know how they are derived. It is very unfortunate that a good portion of the people in the credit business and financial industry (so-called experts) do not even know how the bureaus come up with the scores.

Actually – Credit scores are designed to show the likelihood that the borrower will become 90 days late or delinquent on an account within the next 24 months. Credit score are predictors of the future probabilities based on current and past performance.

Scores divide borrowers up into ten different cards or models. We are not going to get into what the different models are or the categories as it is not necessary for our purposes.

What we do want to know is how the scores are put together and what is important in their calculations. So, what we are going to do is take a look at what is important to the credit scores and how much impact each aspect has in determining the scores.

What are the Important Factors in Calculating My Credit Score?

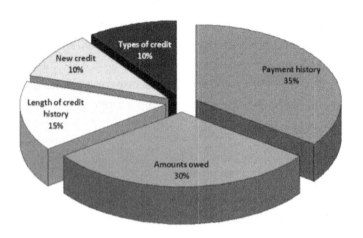

- **35% = Payment History**

- **30% = Amount, i.e. Proportion of Balance to Limits**

- **15% = Credit History**

- **10% = Types of Credit**

- **10% = Credit Inquiries**

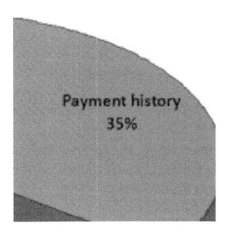

First and foremost is **Payment History.** How you make your payments in relation to the due dates on your accounts is the basis for **35%** of your credit score. When looking at late payments they look at the recency, frequency and severity of the payment history. The importance of each is broken down even further.

Recency of late payments is divided into three categories. First and most important is how many late payments have you had in the last six months?

The next category being how many late payments you've had between seven and twenty-three months ago. It is also next in importance.

The third category is how many late payments you've had more than 24 months ago. This last category doesn't have near the effect the first two categories have but it is still on your report.

Frequency of late payments is the number of times you have been late on each account and on how many of your accounts. Obviously if you have one late account you will be in better shape than if all of your accounts have been paid late.

Severity of your late payments are just that. How late were you – 30 days, 60 days, 90 days or 120 + days? The further behind you are the lower your credit score will be.

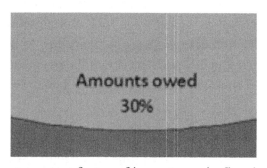

The next greatest factor of importance in figuring out credit scores, are the **Amounts** that you owe. That is the balances of your accounts. **30%** of your overall score is due directly to the amount and proportion of your balances. Ideal balances are between about 30% – 40% or less of your total credit limit on your accounts for revolving accounts (credit cards in particular).

If your balance gets over 50% of your credit limit your scores are hit pretty hard. Any amounts over 75% are hit really hard as far as your score is concerned. High balances are a very good indicator of the potential for becoming 90 days late.

The overall combined credit limits and balances are considered. Example: If you have five - $5000 limit credit cards (a total of $25,000 of available credit) and have a balance on one of them of $5000 then you are at 20% of your total available limit. On the other hand, if you have one $5000 limit card and you have a $4000 balance you are at 80%. Now your score will be taking a beating.

Keep in mind that the proportion is more important than the total amount. If you have a $100 revolving credit limit and your balance is $90 you are at 90%. The dollar amount does not really matter.

Note: Installment loans (auto, mortgages, etc.) are not considered with proportion of balance to limits. They are factored differently – mainly by payment history, age and type of account.

HELOC's (Home Equity Line of Credit) are looked at like an installment loan even though many of them give you a line of credit that you may draw from like a revolving account. Again, payment history and age will carry more weight with these types of accounts.

Length of credit history
15%

Credit History accounts for **15%** of your total score. The age of the oldest trade lines and the number of new trade lines are the two most important factors considered. You will score considerably lower if you have a lot of new trade lines than if you have some that are many years old.

How many accounts should you have? Experts disagree on the ideal number of accounts. Many say 3 to 5 revolving accounts are good. It appears that the quality of the account means more than the actual number. That is: how it's been paid, the age and type of the account and the proportion of balance in regard to limit.

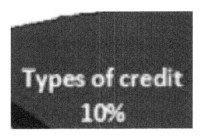

Types of credit
10%

10% of your score is related to the **Type of Credit** Accounts you carry. There are positive trade lines and negative trade lines. Positive accounts include mortgages, auto loans, certain installment loans and credit cards (if they're bank issued).

Negative accounts can be Finance Company loans, Store issued credit cards (usually caused by the high proportion of balance to limits), PayDay loans, car title loans, as well as many others. These are all good indicators that a consumer has a very good probability of becoming ninety days late within the next twenty-four months.

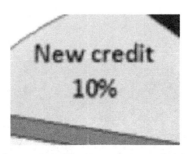

And **10%** of your credit score has to do with the number of Credit **Inquiries** you have on your credit report. What is looked at is the number of inquiries you have had in the last 12 months. Inquiries actually stay on your credit report for 24 months although they are not much of a factor after twelve months.

Credit Inquiries count a maximum of about five to seven inquiries each, representing between 5 and 15 points each off of your score.

Mortgage and Auto inquiries do not count against you if they are in a thirty-day period. They do give you a "window" for shopping. But if you're out shopping for cars every month of the year it will count against you.

You do not want to have a lot of unnecessary credit inquiries on your credit report. You can appear to be desperate for credit. It is looked at as very unfavorable.

BAD		FAIR	GOOD	BEST
300		640	680	720	850

Where are you in regard to everyone else?

How do you rank in credit scores with the rest of Americans? Recently the average credit score across the country was 720. Which means half the people had a score greater than 720 and half of the people had a score below 720.

What do I need to have a FICO/credit score?

Remember... in order to even get a credit score you need these three things:

1) You must have a trade line at least six months old.

2) You must have at least one trade line updated at the bureau within the last six months.

3) The Social Security number you are using cannot be associated with the terrorist list or a dead person.

Who Comes Up with this Stuff?

Chapter 3: Who Comes Up with this Stuff? How? Why?

Chapter 3

Who Comes Up with This Stuff? How? Why?

"They say that marriages are made in Heaven. But so is thunder and lightning."
~Clint Eastwood~

Who reports the information to the credit bureaus?

This may seem a bit confusing. So, let's simplify it. It works something like this. The three main credit bureaus are given information, usually on a monthly basis, from the credit reporting agencies (CRAs).

This information includes your account information such as balances, payment history, etc. They also report information such as collection activities on overdue bills. The bureaus also receive information from public records.

The CRAs in turn get their information from the three credit bureaus and put it in an organized format that should be somewhat decipherable to you.

How long does the information stay on your credit report? As already stated, credit inquiries stay on your credit report for two years even though they only count against your score for the previous twelve months.

Information on your credit accounts stay on your report for seven years regardless if the information is positive or negative.

A Summary of Your Rights Under the Fair Credit Reporting Act

The federal Fair Credit Reporting Act (FCRA) is designed to promote accuracy, fairness, and privacy of information in the files of every "consumer reporting agency" (CRA).

Most CRA's are credit bureaus that gather and sell information about you – such as if you pay your bills on time or have filed bankruptcy – to creditors, employers, landlords, and other businesses.

You can find the complete text of the FCRA, 15 U.S.C. 1681 – 1681u, at the Federal Trade commission's web site (http://www.ftc.gov). The FCRA gives you specific rights, as outlined below.

You may have additional rights under state law. You may contact a state or local consumer protection agency or state attorney general to learn those rights.

You must be told if information in your file has been used against you. Anyone who uses information from a CRA to take action against you – such as denying an application for credit, insurance, or employment – must tell you, and give you the name, address, and phone number of the CRA that provided the consumer report.

You can find out what is in your file. At your request, a CRA must give you the information in your file, and a list of everyone who has requested it recently. There is no charge for the report if a person has taken action against you because of information supplied by the CRA, if you request the information within sixty days of receiving notice of the action.

You are also entitled to one free report every twelve months upon request if you certify that (1) you are unemployed and plan to seek employment within 60 days, (2) you are on welfare, or (3) your report is inaccurate due to fraud. Otherwise, a CRA may charge you eight dollars.

You can dispute inaccurate information with the CRA. If you tell a CRA that your file contains inaccurate information, the CRA must investigate the terms (usually within 30 days) by presenting to its information source all relevant evidence you submit, unless your dispute is frivolous.

The source must review your evidence and report its findings to the CRA. (The source must also advise national CRAs – to which it has provided the data – of any error.) The CRA must give you a written report of the investigation and a copy of your report if the investigation results in any change.

If the CRA's investigation does not resolve the dispute, you may add a brief statement to your file. The CRA must normally include a summary of your statement in future reports.

If an item is deleted or a dispute statement is filed, you may ask that anyone who has recently received your report be notified of the change.

Inaccurate information must be corrected or deleted. A CRA must remove or correct inaccurate or unverified information from its files, usually within 30 days after you dispute it. However, the CRA is not required to remove accurate data from your file unless it is outdated (as described below) or cannot be verified.

If your dispute results in any change to your report, the CRA cannot reinsert into your file a disputed item unless the information source verifies its accuracy and completeness. In addition, the CRA must give you a written notice telling you it has reinserted the item. The notice must include the name, address and phone number of the information source.

You can dispute inaccurate items with the source of the information. If you tell anyone – such as a creditor who reports to a CRA – that you dispute an item, they may not then report the information to a CRA without including a notice of your dispute. In addition, once you've notified the source of the error in writing, it may not continue to report the information if it is, in fact, an error.

Outdated information may not be reported. In most cases, a CRA may not report negative information that is more than seven years old; ten years for bankruptcies.

Access to your file is limited. A CRA may provide information about you only to people with a need recognized by the FCRA – usually to consider an application with a creditor, insurer, employer, landlord, or other business.

Your consent is required for reports that are provided to employers, or reports that contain medical information. A CRA may not give out information about you to your employer, or prospective employer without your written consent.

A CRA may not report medical information about you to creditors, insurers, or employers without your permission.

You may choose to exclude your name from CRA list for unsolicited credit and insurance offers. Creditors and insurers may use file information as the basis for sending you unsolicited offers of credit or insurance.

Such offers must include a toll-free phone number for you to call if you want your name and address removed from future lists. If you call, you must be kept off the list for two years. If you request, complete, and return the CRA form provided for this purpose, you must be taken off the list indefinitely.

You may seek damages from violators. If a CRA, a user or (in some cases) a provider of CRA data, violates the FCRA, you may sue them in state or federal court.

The FCRA gives several different federal agencies authority to enforce the FCRA:

For questions or concerns regarding: CRAs, creditors and others not listed below

Please contact: Federal Trade Commission – Consumer Response Center – FCRA Washington, DC 20580 * 202- 326-3761

Regarding: National banks, federal branches/agencies of foreign banks (word "National" or initials "N.A." appear in or after bank's name)

Contact: Office of the Comptroller of the Currency Compliance Management, Mail Stop 6-6 Washington, DC 20219 * 800-613-6743

Regarding: Federal Reserve System member banks (except national banks, and federal branches/agencies of foreign banks)

Contact: Federal Reserve Board Division of Consumer & Community Affairs Washington, DC 20551 * 202-452- 3693

Regarding: Savings associations and federally chartered savings banks (word "Federal" or initials "F.S.B." appear in federal institution's name)

Contact: Office of Thrift Supervision Consumer Programs, Washington, DC 20552 * 800-842-6929

Regarding: Federal Credit Unions (word "Federal Credit Union" appear in institution's name)

Contact: National Credit Union Administration 1775 Duke Street Alexandria, VA 22314 * 703-518-6360

Regarding: State-chartered banks that are not members of the Federal Reserve System

Contact: Federal Deposit Insurance Corporation Division of Compliance & Consumer Affairs Washington, DC 20429 * 800-934-FDIC

Regarding: Air, surface, or rail common carriers regulated by former Civil Aeronautics Board or Interstate Commerce Commission

Contact: Department of Transportation Office of Financial Management Washington, DC 20590 * 202-366-1306

Regarding: Activities subject to the Packers and Stockyards Act, 1921

Contact: Department of Agriculture Office of Deputy Administrator – GIPSA Washington, DC 20250 * 202- 720-7051

Who is Saying What About Me?

Chapter 4: Who is Saying What About Me?

Chapter 4

Who is Saying What About Me & Why?

Are they saying that O is the last letter of
Zero or the first letter of Opportunity?

Who Reports My Information?

The Three Major Credit Reporting Bureaus are:

Experian

701 Experian Parkway
P.O. Box 4500
Allen TX 75013*
1.888.397.3742

Trans Union

2 Baldwin Place
P.O. Box 1000
Chester PA 19022 *
1.800.916.8800

Equifax

P.O. Box 740256
Atlanta, GA 30374*
1.800.685.1111

*These addresses and phone numbers are current as of publication. They do change from time to time. It is recommended you verify the information before corresponding.

What information is on your credit report?

What information *can* be put into your credit report? As mentioned earlier some of things they can actually put in your credit file are:

Payment history - how you've paid your accounts. Outstanding debt – balances and credit limits. Credit history – age of your trade lines.

Inquiries and *new accounts* opened – who has been looking at your credit report. How many inquiries you have had in the last two years. What accounts have you opened in the last year?

Types of credit accounts in use – number of trade lines reported for each type of account, i.e. bankcards, department store cards, finance company accounts, installment loans, auto loans, home mortgages, etc.

What is not reported to the credit bureaus and also cannot be used in determining your credit score?

Scores *do not* use race, color, religion, national origin, sex, marital status, or age as predictive characteristics. Occupation and length of time at present residence are also not used in the scorecards. Any other information that is not present in a credit file is not used in creating a credit bureau score.

The following are the explanations that are used from the various bureaus with respect to the factors used in determining how they arrived at the score.

Experian – FICO score

Factor Definition

. 01 Amount owed on accounts is too high

. 02 Level of delinquency on accounts

. 03 Too few bank revolving accounts

. 04 Too many bank or national revolving accounts

. 05 Too many accounts with balances

. 06 Too many consumer finance accounts

. 07 Account payment history is too new to rate

. 08 Number of recent inquiries

   33 Proportion of current loan balance to original loan amount

. 09 Number of accounts opened within the last twelve months

. 10 Proportion of balance to high credit on bank

revolving or all revolving accounts

- 11 Current balances on revolving accounts

- 12 Length of revolving account history

- 13 Length of time (or unknown time) since account delinquencies

- 14 Length of time accounts have been established

- 15 Insufficient or lack of bank revolving account information

- 16 Insufficient or lack of revolving account information

- 17 No recent (non-mortgage) account balance information

- 18 Number of accounts delinquent

- 19 Too few accounts rated "current"

- 20 Time since derogatory public record or collection too short

- 21 Amount past due on accounts

- 22 Serious delinquencies, derogatory public record or collections filed

- 23 Number of bank or national revolving accounts

with balances

. 24 No recent revolving balances

27 Too few accounts currently paid as agreed

29 No recent bank card balances

. 30 Time since most recent account opening is too short

32 No recent installment loan information

. 38 Serious delinquency and public record or collection filed

. 39 Serious delinquency

. 40 Derogatory public record or collection filed

26 Number of revolving accounts

28 Number of accounts established

37 Number of finance company accounts established relative to length of finance history

99 Lack of recent information on finance accounts, or lack of finance accounts

TransUnion – Empirica score

. 00 No adverse factors

- 01 Amount owed on accounts is too high

- 02 Level of delinquency on accounts

- 03 Proportion of loan balances to loan amounts is too high

- 04 Insufficient installment credit history

- 05 Too many accounts with balances

- 06 Too many consumer finance accounts with balances

- 07 Account payment history is too new to rate

- 08 Too many inquiries within the last 12 months

- 09 Too many accounts recently opened

- 10 Proportion of balance to limits too high on revolving accounts

- 11 Excessive amount owed on revolving accounts

- 12 Length of time revolving accounts have been established

- 13 Delinquency date too recent, or unknown

- 14 Length of time accounts have been established

- 15 Lack of recent bank revolving information

. 16 Lack of recent revolving account information

. 17 No recent non-mortgage balance information

. 18 Number of accounts with delinquencies

. 19 Date of last inquiry too recent

. 20 Time since derogatory public record or collection too short

. 21 Amount past due on accounts

. 22 Serious delinquency, derogatory public record or collections filed

24 No recent revolving balances

. 27 Too few accounts currently paid as agreed

. 28 Number of established accounts

. 29 No recent bank card balances

. 30 Time since most recent account opening is too short

. 31 Amount owed on delinquent accounts

. 38 Serious delinquency and public record or collection filed

. 39 Serious delinquency

- 40 Derogatory public record or collection filed

- 97 Lack of recent auto loan information

- 98 Length of time consumer finance co. loans have been established

Equifax- Beacon/Pinnacle score

- 01 Amount owed on accounts is too high

- 02 Level of delinquency on accounts

- 04 Too many bank or national revolving/open accounts

- 05 Too many accounts with balances

- 06 Too many consumer finance accounts

- 07 Account payment history is too new to rate

- 08 Too many inquiries within the last twelve months

- 09 Too many accounts recently opened

- 10 Proportion of balance to limits too high on revolving accounts

- 11 Amounts owed on revolving accounts too high

- 12 Length of time revolving/open accounts have

been established

- 13 Time since delinquency too recent or unknown

- 14 Length of time accounts have been established

- 15 Lack of recent bank revolving information

- 16 Lack of recent revolving account information

- 17 No recent non-mortgage balance information

- 18 Number of accounts with delinquencies

- 19 Too few accounts currently paid as agreed

- 20 Time since derogatory public record or collection too short

- 21 Amount past due on accounts

- 22 Serious delinquent/derogatory public record or collections filed

- 23 Number of bank or national revolving accounts with balances

- 24 No recent revolving balances

28 Number of established accounts

- 30 Time since most recent account opening is too short

- 31 Too few accounts with recent payment information

- 32 Lack of recent installment loan information

- 33 Proportion of loan balances or loan amounts too high

- 34 Amount owed on delinquent accounts

- 38 Serious delinquency and public record or collection filed

- 39 Serious delinquency

- 40 Derogatory public record or collection filed

The way the codes will appear on your credit report will look something like this:

FOR: DOE, JOHN Q. 555-55-5555 XPN FAIR
ISAAC RISK SCORE: 669 COMMENTS: 40
DEROGATORY PUBLIC RECORD OR
COLLECTION FILED

FOR: TUC COMMENTS:

COLLECTION

DOE, JOHN Q. 555-55-5555 EMPIRICA SCORE:
675

COMMENTS: PUBLIC

00038 SERIOUS DELINQUENCY, AND DEROGATORY

RECORD OR COLLECTION FILED 00014 LENGTH OF TIME ACCOUNTS HAVE BEEN

ESTABLISHED 00008 TOO MANY INQUIRIES WITHIN THE LAST TWELVE

MONTHS 00020 LENGTH OF TIME SINCE DEROGATORY PUBLIC

RECORD OR COLLECTION IS TOO SHORT

10 PROPORTION OF BALANCE TO HIGH CREDIT ON BANK

REVOLVING OR ALL REVOLVING ACCOUNTS 14 LENGTH OF TIME ACCOUNTS HAVE BEEN ESTABLISHED 08 NUMBER OF RECENT INQUIRIES

038 SERIOUS DELINQUENCY, AND PUBLIC RECORD OR COLLECTION FILED 020 RECENT DROGATORY PUBLIC RECORD OR

008 TOO MANY RECENT CREDIT CHECKS 14 INSUFFICIENT LENGTH OF CREDIT HISTORY

FOR: DOE, JOHN Q. 555-55-5555 EFX FACTA BEACON 5.0 SCORE: 689

As you can see the credit bureaus will actually tell you why they came up with the score that they did. After this they usually have your accounts listed. Some reporting agencies will list the derogatory and delinquent accounts first and some will list them with accounts that are paid as agreed.

They will usually tell you the type of account and the account number, which bureau it is being reported at, the date the account was opened, the date last reported to the bureau and how the account is being paid. It will also usually say when the account was paid off if it is closed and any actions taken such as collections and write offs.

You report will list the last reported current balance of the account, what the high credit limit is or what the original loan amount was and the monthly payment. Any past due amounts will be shown here, too.

If any accounts are currently with collection agencies, they should have the original creditor listed as well.

The bureaus use a lot of coded information or shortcuts such as M-1 or I-5 or R-1. Don't let these confuse or intimidate you. Just about all of the industries in today's society use some kind of abbreviations and acronyms and the credit people are no different. They can be easily learned.

The M represents a mortgage account. The I is an installment account. And the R stands for a revolving account. The number following the letter is reporting how the account has been or is being paid. The 1's are showing the account as being paid as agreed and the 9's meaning the accounts are very derogatory.

Public records will normally be listed either before your credit accounts or after them. Public records will consist of any kind of judgments against you with the latest status.

Bankruptcies will be shown here including the type, when filed, the docket number and the disposition (that is if it is dismissed or in progress).

Any tax liens and judgments you may have as well as child support owed will also usually be in this section.

The next section will be the inquiries. It is required that anyone who looks at your credit report for any reason to be on record. It shows the bureau they inquired with, the date of the inquiry, their file number and who they are. This information stays on your credit report for a period of two years.

Additional information that is on your credit report will be the credit bureaus contact information, which includes the name, address and phone numbers.

Also, the creditor contact information must be posted on your credit report. Anyone who puts any information on your credit report is required by law to list his or her name, address and phone number.

There is usually a section on the report for variations in your name and a social security number check. Most often they will have your current address and maybe some of your previous addresses where you have lived. In addition, your employer may also be listed. This information is not always current and up to date.

At the end of the credit report there will be a section that shows totals. It will list the number of public records and inquiries; how many accounts are paid as agreed and how many are delinquent.

Also shown are the kinds of accounts listed on the report, whether they are installment, revolving, real estate or other accounts. It will also state the balances, the amount of the payments and any amounts that are past due. It's basically a summary of your credit report in a nutshell.

Not all credit reports are in this exact format. All the information needs to be listed but some are shown in different formats. The reason for this is there are many different reporting agencies.

There are only three credit bureaus but there are many agencies that report the information and they all have their own style of reporting.

How Much Money can I $ave Now?

Chapter 5: How Much Money can I $ave Now?

Chapter 5

How Much Money can I $ave Now?

"If *Saving* money is wrong, I don't want to be right." ~William Shatner~

Everything can cost less with a better credit score.

You Will Save Big $$$ with a Good Credit score! You Will also have Many More Options!

- **Better Interest Rates**

- **Lower Insurance Premiums**

- **More Favorable for Employers**

- **Choose Who You want to Do Business with**

- **Many More Choices**

According to myFICO.com as you improve your scores, you will pay less when you buy on credit – whether you're purchasing a home, cell phone, automobile or signing up for credit cards.

Better Interest Rates

Here an example we used earlier of a $150,000 30-year, fixed-rate mortgage:

The *Difference* Can Be *Substantial*

- **With a Lower Score ~ $150,000** @ 7% - 360 months = **$997.95**/month

- Total = **$359,263.35**

- **With a Higher Score ~ $150,000** @ 4% - 360 months = **$716.12**/month

- Total = **$257,804.26**

- Difference = **$281.83**/month

- Total Savings = **$101,459.09**

As you can see there's a tremendous amount of difference in how much you'll pay based upon your credit score. Other credit accounts are similar in respect to the interest they charge in regard to your score.

Lower Insurance Premiums

Insurance premiums are also affected.

What about insurance rates? In the last couple of years many insurance companies have started using credit scores to determine the rates you will pay on your insurance premiums.

They say that a person with a lower credit score is more likely to file a claim than a person with a higher score. Sound absurd? They're doing it. Could it be that they just lost a lot of money in the 1990's in the stock market and 2000's in real estate? This could be a good way to recoup some of those losses.

It used to be that an insurance company would run credit checks and investigations only if you were applying for a large amount of life insurance and for certain property and casualty insurance.

Nowadays most companies are pulling credit reports for regular homeowners and car insurance. The difference in the premiums can be staggering.

Let's look at some examples.

- **_Homeowners Insurance_**, _perhaps the same $150,000 mortgage shown earlier*_

- High Score = **$700**/year

- Low Score = **$1200**/year

- Difference Savings of **$500**/year = **$15,000**/30 years

- **_Auto Insurance*_**

- High Score = **$1200**/year - Low Score = **$2400**/year

- Difference Savings of **$1200**/year = **$36,000**/30 years

*In all fairness there are many other factors considered with insurance premiums such as zip codes-deductibles-endorsements-liability, etc. Always check with your insurance professional.

Credit scores are just one more way your premiums can be adjusted, higher or lower.

You will pay less for other loans as well.

What about automobile loans and credit cards? You guessed it. Credit scores also affect these interest rates.

Today just about anyone can get an auto loan and some type of credit card no matter how low your credit score is and regardless of your history. The difference in the rates can be overwhelming.

The financial industry calls these higher rate programs "alternative" credit. With a lower credit score you are looked at as a higher risk to loan money to and you will pay a much higher rate accordingly.

Much More Favorable for Employers

Many Employers check your credit reports as part of their background check. It can be the difference in getting hired or not getting hired.

I recently read that over fifty percent of potential employers use your credit rating when considering you for employment. This is second only to your social media profiles such as *twitter* and *facebook*.

Not only is it a good idea to not post incriminating things on the Internet, you also want employers to see your good credit report.

Choose Who You Want to do Business with!

You Have Many More Choices!

By having a good credit score you have many more choices of who *you* want to do business with. Many times, with a lower credit score you are considered a *high* credit risk and are limited who chooses to do business with you.

There are so many benefits you give yourself by having a high credit score. It's a really good feeling to know that you do not have all of the limitations that those with a low score have.

With a high credit score you can pretty much control your finances and your financial future. Just a little education can completely change your life.

Where Can I Find Out About ME How Much is This Going to Cost ME?

Chapter 6: Where Can I Find Out About ME? How Much is This Going to Cost ME?

Chapter 6

Where Can I Find Out About ME? How Much is This Going to Cost ME?

"If you don't get lost, there's a chance you will never be found." ~Anonymous~

Where Can I Find Out About Me?

How can *I* get a copy of *my* credit report and get started?

Before you can increase your credit worthiness you must first find out where you are right now. You need to get a copy of your credit report from credit report with the scores.

Where do you get copies of your credit reports? There are many sources these days. It is a lot easier than it used to be. Are there places to get them that are better than others? Perhaps. Recently the advertisements have sprung up all over the place.

How much can they charge ME for a report?

According to FCRA (the federal "Fair Credit Reporting Act") they can charge up to $8 for a credit report. How much do they charge? I've seen everything up to $49.95 and much more for three reports with the scores. Many companies have membership sites now and charge an on-going monthly fee of $10 to $60+. How do they get away with this? Good question.

Okay, Where Do I Start?

According to **FCRA** (Fair Credit Reporting Act) you are entitled to a *free* copy of your credit report if you are denied credit and make a request within 30 days.

Back in the day I used this several times to get a copy of my credit report. Before I knew any better I thought that any time I want to get a copy of my credit report I would just apply for something I knew that I would not get approved for.

A Free Credit Report just because I was denied credit? Good idea? Or *Not* such a good idea? Unnecessary Inquiries can be derogatory. Much more on this in a later chapter.

Today is quite a bit different from when I used to get a *free* credit report because I was denied credit. Today we have almost instant access to a lot of information. So, where did I go to look for a *free* credit report? I went to Google.

Here's what Google had to say:

Amazing within 0.19 seconds they came up with 296,000,000 results! Well I wasn't going to go through all two hundred and ninety-six million sites.

So, I decided to go through a couple of the ones that many of us are familiar with. These are only a few of the many sites that are available.

I am not endorsing, condoning or condemning any of these sites. There are some good things about these sites and should be used at your own discretion. Be aware of the fine print and make sure it is in your best interest.

I looked at three of the most popular sites. There are many more. The three I checked out are:

- FreeCreditReport.com

- AnnualCreditReport.com

- CreditKarma.com

FreeCreditReport.com

Free Credit Report dot com is a site that is advertised on television quite a bit. Sounds like a good thing. *Free* is always good, right? Well, like anything, it's best to go in with your eyes wide open.

Here's what I found out:

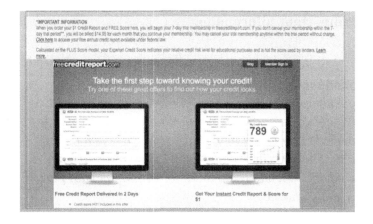

It is a little hard to see some of this even though I enlarged the print. A couple of things I noticed were kind of interesting. On the first page they had two choices.

The first choice was your *free* credit report delivered in 2 days. Credit score NOT included in this offer.

The second choice was your instant credit report & score for $1. Well, doesn't sound too bad. Instant gratification for only one dollar. Okay. Only $1.

Then I looked at the fine print. In fact, I enlarged the fine print and it's still a little small for me to read. This is what it says:

*Important Information

*When you order your $1 Credit Report and FREE Score here, you will begin your 7-day trial membership in freecreditreport.com If you don't cancel your membership within the 7-day trial period**, you will be billed $14.99 for each month that you continue your membership. You may cancel your trial membership anytime within the trial period without charge.*

Click here to access your free annual credit report available under federal law.

Calculated on the PLUS score model, your Experian Credit Score indicates your relative credit risk level for education purposes and is not the score used by lenders.

What does all of this mean? Well it looks as if you can get your credit report instantly with the score for only $1. It also looks like to get this information right now I need to pay a dollar with a credit card.

Why do I need a membership for $14.99 each month to get my credit report and score now? I'm not really sure that I need a membership and my experience is that I usually forget to cancel them with-in the *trial period*.

I'm also wondering why my score is calculated on the PLUS score model for educational purposes only and not the score used by lenders. I chose not to get the membership for only $14.99 each month.

One thing that did get my attention was part that said:

Click here to access your free annual credit report available under federal law.

So, I clicked here. It took me to:

AnnualCreditReport.com

AnnualCredit**Report**.com
The only source for your free credit reports. Authorized by Federal law.

This site will give you a free credit report of all three bureaus once a year. You do have to pay for the scores. I thought, okay I'm game. Let's get a free credit report.

It was quite an ordeal to set up an account. I do not have a problem giving information that only I know when it comes to keeping my financial well-being secure.

The information that I had to give was about as much, if not more, than any loan I have ever applied for. That's okay. Not everyone would know everything about me.

Some of the info was pretty deep. I'm not sure why they wanted to know my great-great-great grandmother's maiden name and the name of the boat she came over on (just kidding). It really was a lot of information.

All right, no problem. I got my account set up and was ready to get my three credit reports and *buy* the scores. So, I got right to it.

It wasn't that I just got the reports and scores easily. Each report required another whole set of questions and answers. Well, I was the only one that would know my information. Right? So, I thought.

The first credit report from Experian I received with no problem after my *interrogation*. Lots and lots of questions. I did get the report. Still no score, which I will have to pay for.

The second report from Transunion was not so easily obtained. After the questions and *interrogation,* I was told that I could not get my report because I didn't answer all of the questions correctly.

The third report from Equifax was about the same as Transunion. Nada. Apparently, I do not know enough information about myself two out of three times.

I couldn't even figure out what else they wanted to know. The only thing I could think of was maybe I didn't connect a right address with a mortgage loan. I do have several in several different towns. It didn't make a lot of sense to me.

They did offer a phone number I could call and an address I could write to get my *free* reports. I chose not to waste any more of my time. I was already into to this way more than I cared to be after setting up *my account*.

There was one other site where I did get a *free* copy of my credit report with a credit score. That is:

CreditKarma.com

Credit ⬤ Karma   Credit Cards   Loans   Reviews   Tools & Advice

I first heard about Credit Karma a few years ago at a *Dean Graziosi* real estate event. This is a pretty good site that appears to be *truly free*. It has limited information and is a snapshot of your credit report with the score.

It is *not* a tri-merge report used by lenders for issuing credit. It is still a good site with current information. As far as I can tell they make their money on offers to you from their advertisers.

They do not hound you or bother you with unsolicited offers and spam emails. If you choose, they will send you a quarterly reminder to check your updated report, with the score.

The sign-up process was simple. They asked for some personal information that only I would know. It was very basic, and I *knew* all of the questions.
Not only did I not have to give my ancestors maiden names, I didn't even enter my full social security number. It was a very easy enrollment process.

So far, I have had a member profile and used their services for a few years and have not spent any money. This site has been a good source for personal credit information with a score at no cost to me. This seems to be a truly *free* service.

Traditional FREE Credit Reports

There are a few other ways to get a *free* credit report. You can apply for a loan with your local bank. If you own a home, you can talk to them about refinancing your mortgage.

If you do not own a home, you might apply for home loan to see what your possibilities are of obtaining a mortgage. By applying for a mortgage, they will pull all three credit reports with the scores.

A good loan officer or mortgage broker will go over your report with you. You can ask and they may or may not give you a copy. If they don't give you a copy, just take some notes.
Car dealers and loan companies are some other sources where you may be able to apply for credit and find out about your ability to borrow.

Be aware that you do *not* want a lot of unnecessary *hard* credit inquiries (specific details about this later on improving your credit score). Inquiries can actually hurt your score if you have too many.

There are many more sources to get a personal credit report. Just be aware of some of the consequences and *programs* you may be signing up for. Always read the fine print and see what the real *catch* may be.

What if I Already Dropped Off the Deep End...with...Bankruptcy-Foreclosure-Repossessions-Collections-Judgments-Tax Liens-Public Records-Child Support?

Chapter 7: What if I Already Dropped Off the Deep End…with…

Bankruptcy-Foreclosure-Repossessions-Collections-Judgments-Tax Liens-Public Records-Child Support?

Chapter 7

What if I Already Dropped Off of the Deep End…with…Bankruptcy-Foreclosure-Repossession-Collections-Judgments-Tax Liens-Public Records-Child Support?

"Forgiveness says *You* are given another chance to a new beginning." ~Desmond Tutu~

Bankruptcy

What if you already filed or have gone through a **Bankruptcy**? Sometimes a bankruptcy may be the best way out of your financial dilemma and needs to be considered carefully.

Always consult with competent council. Laws change frequently and you need to have good up-to-date advisors. Choose your legal counsel wisely.

There are two types of personal bankruptcies. There is a chapter 13 which is a repayment plan and a chapter 7 which is a debt elimination program.

You may be thinking why not just file a chapter 7 and get rid of the debts all together? Some debts may not be able to be discharged. Student loans are one example.

Student loans are government guaranteed loans that must be paid back regardless of a bankruptcy. You may be able to put them into a chapter 13.

A chapter 13 bankruptcy is a repayment plan. In some cases, it may be best for you to regroup and have the court come up with a plan for you to pay back your creditors with a new payment schedule.

Of course, you will need a bankruptcy attorney and some good counseling. It must be considered wisely.

Bankruptcies will stay on your credit report for ten (10) years from the time of discharge. This is regardless of whether you have filed a chapter 7 or a chapter 13.

Initially bankruptcies usually have a very negative effect on your credit score. In the long run it may actually have a more positive effect than where you may have been before.

I've seen many that have gone through a chapter 7 elimination plan establish new accounts with a good fresh start. You are very limited with the creditors that will do business with you.

You will also pay more money in fees and higher interest rates during and after your bankruptcy. It just depends on how much you want to get your finances back in order. Sometimes the cost of rebuilding your credit is not as important as the result.

With a chapter 13 repayment plan you may actually be able to improve your score while you are repaying your debts. Usually it has a very negative effect at the outset.

By making your payments through the court, and on time, your score should go up. I've seen many people that could get a home loan right after their bankruptcy was discharged.

The other side of the coin is that if you do not make your payments and do not make them on time, your score could get way lower. Your payment history with the court will make a huge difference.

Foreclosure & Short Sales

You hear a lot about **Foreclosures and Short Sales** these days. The real estate in the United States has had some major adjustments in the last few years. Many of us have been affected in some way by a foreclosure or a short sale.

A foreclosure is exactly that. If you don't pay your mortgage for a period of time, the lender will foreclose on the property and retake possession.

Traditionally a good rule of thumb was that if you didn't make your mortgage payments for three months, they would start foreclosure proceedings.

Today is a little bit different. I've seen people stay in their homes for a couple of years without making a payment. Why are the lenders waiting so long? I guess they would rather have someone in the house than an empty house.

Short sales are more common today than they used to be. A short sale is where the lender agrees to sell the home for less than what is owed on the loan. Why would they do that?

In the last few years we have had some pretty big corrections in real estate in most parts of the country. The homes do not have the value that they were once valued at. The lenders would rather get most of their money than to go through a foreclosure process.

The homeowners in many cases want to preserve their credit. Let's face it. Our life situations do change from time to time. There are divorces, deaths, illnesses, inheritances, remarriages, extended families, upsizing, downsizing and the reasons are endless.

Foreclosures and Short Sales will stay on your credit report for seven (7) years. The longer the time period from the time the foreclosure or short sale is posted on your credit report the less effect it will have on your score.

Many lenders will not extend credit to those with a foreclosure or a short sale. There are lenders that will extend credit. You can expect to pay more fees and a higher interest rate as well.

Repossessions & Collections

Repossessions and collections will stay on your credit report for seven (7) years. The longer period of time since they are reported the less affect they will have on your score.

Repossessions will occur if you fail to make your payments on things like auto loans, furniture, appliances, etc. Usually if you become three (3) months in arrears on your payments, they will send someone out for your/their merchandise.

Repossessions can be really nasty. Most creditors will simply add a derogatory entry on your credit report. Others will come after you for the money. They may have gotten the merchandise back. They may attach lots of money in added fees and collection costs.

What about a *voluntary repossession?* Voluntary repossessions can be as derogatory as an *involuntary* repossession. There are some companies out there that will tell you to just give back the car (or whatever) back.

Many will say they will give you credit for the amount that they get for your car. Many times, you may be told that they only got a fraction of the amount that you actually owed. You can owe the difference.

The creditor may say they got two thousand for your car when in fact your car note still had a balance of ten thousand. They may send the eight-thousand-dollar balance to a *collector.*

Collections and repossessions can go hand in hand. Collections can also be associated with many types of unpaid bills including medical bills. The amount of the collection does not matter as much as how recent they are as far as your score goes.

Collection companies can be a nightmare to deal with. We've all heard the stories of the debt collector calling during dinner, calling at work and all kinds of other inconvenient times. Well we should be paying our obligations.

Many collection companies will add on all kinds of *fees* to the original amount of the debt. Many will tack on things like auction fees, restocking fees, interest, new collection fees, attorney and legal fees to name just a few.

As time goes on the collection will not have as much factor on your credit score. It will have a tremendous effect on your score if they keep it updated. If the collector updates it regularly it can have an impact for several years.

Today there are many collection companies that *buy and sell* collection accounts. There are some things to be aware of when your account changes hands.

I have seen many accounts that have been sold, updated and duplicated. *Duplicated?* Yes duplicated. It can be a little confusing and a pain to deal with. Many times, they can be dealt with.

When accounts are sold, they may be duplicated on your credit report. It works something like this.

You have an account with XYZ company for $10,000 that you default on. After several months of attempting to collect the debt from you they give up. At this point your balance may be $12,500 with added fees.

They might write this off as a profit and loss. They sell this *nonperforming* account to another more aggressive collection company ABC at a discount. ABC adds their fees and attempt to collect the debt that may now be $15,600. If they're not successful in collecting form, you they may sell your account again.

QRX company comes along and buys your account from ABC. Again, they buy at a discount. After taking over your collection account they will add their fees. You may be up to a total of $17,200.

Even though this is only one account, it may show up on your credit report all three times. Old collections are not necessarily replaced or associated with each other.

Your credit report may report all three collections with different account numbers and different amounts. The reporting bureau may have no way of knowing the accounts are one in the same.

Many collection companies come and go. Many change hands, merge and are bought out themselves. They can be difficult to track down when you are trying to improve your score.

Judgments

Judgments will show up on your credit report when you are in default through court orders against you. Any time a Judge from a court of law issues a judgment against you it should show up on your credit report.
A judgment can be from an eviction, nonpaid child support, other nonpaid bills or a number of other things that may be ordered from and by a court of law.

A judgment will stay on your credit report for seven (7) years. The longer time period from when it was first reported the less negative effect it will have on your score.

Many lenders will not extend credit based on certain judgments. Many judgments will be required to be paid before issuing credit to you. There are some positive things you can do depending on the situation. More on this later when we are working on improving your credit score.

Tax Liens

Tax liens are what the government will levy against you if you do not pay your taxes. It can be from real estate, personal property, income tax or any other tax you may owe to the government.

If you have a piece of real estate that you do not pay the taxes on, they will put a lien on your property. This lien will go into the first position and must be paid before the mortgage or *any* other lien on the property.

They will also notify the credit bureaus of the levy against you. This will affect your score in a very negative way. You will probably have a very difficult time getting anyone to extend credit to you until this is resolved.

Personal property, income and all other tax delinquencies will also show up on your credit report. They don't go away. The government will get the money you owe them.

Tax liens will remain on your credit report for seven (7) years. As with other negative derogatoriness, they will have less impact on your score with the more time that goes by.

Public Records & Child Support

Public records will show up on your credit report when submitted by the court. They can be anything from an unpaid credit card bill to a grass cutting fee from a municipality where you own a rental or investment property to a traffic ticket.

Child support is very important to pay, and it shows up on your credit report when in arrears. Most child support these days are paid through the court system. They do a very good job of keeping track of what is owed.

There are criminal consequences in addition to credit issues when you do not pay your obligations for your children. Many times, when someone is not paying their child support, they have other issues. The credit score may not be the most important thing right now. Maybe staying out of the slammer might be your immediate concern.

Public records and child support will stay on your credit report for seven (7) years. Time will mend your score unless your information is updated often.

What About THOSE Credit Doctors & Consumer Credit Counseling?

Chapter 8: What About THOSE Credit Doctors & Consumer Credit Counseling?

Chapter 8

What About THOSE Credit Doctors & Consumer Credit Counseling?

Dr. Zira: Taylor! Don't treat him that way!
George Taylor: Why not?
Dr. Zira: It's humiliating!
George Taylor: The way you humiliated me? All of you? YOU led me around on a LEASH!
Cornelius: That was different. We thought you were inferior.
George Taylor: Now you know better.

~Planet of the Apes 1968~

What About THOSE Credit Doctors?

What about all of the clutter out there today about credit repair? You may just want to go to one of *those* companies that can *fix* my credit *now*.

Just about everywhere we turn these days we hear about these magical companies. Many companies sound like they know some mystical secrets of increasing your score by hundreds of points in less than a month.

Some say they can remove all negative things on your credit report. Some say you can start over with a new identity using an EIN number.

Well, I don't want to burst your bubble. There are *No guarantees* when it comes to improving your credit. There are things that you can do that have a good chance of working in your favor. You may also wake up a sleeping dog that have a negative effect on your credit score.

I'm always very interested when I see some of these outrageous guarantees. My experience has shown me that not everything you adjust on your credit report has the outcome you are looking for.

Use extreme caution when considering joining a *credit repair company*. There are a lot of guarantees I am amazed those companies throw out there.

There is a lot of *misinformation* when it comes to credit improvement. I have talked to many of these companies over the years. I'm not sure if they are being deceptive or just really don't know what they are talking about.

I'm sure that most of those *credit-doctor type* companies mean well. Most of the time I do not see what they are offering for the money they charge. Many of the people I talked to at some of those companies got their feathers ruffled when I asked questions.

Recently I decided to check out the *credit doctors* that are out there now. There are more now than ever. For some reason credit scores have gotten very popular. There seems to be a lot of *credit doctors* trying to cash in on what others don't know.

Here's what I found on Google:

It was amazing. Within 0.37 seconds Google came up with 10,200,000 results when I typed in credit repair companies. That's ten million two hundred thousand web pages for credit repair companies.

So next I searched on local web sites. Not quite ten million and still had many. One thing that I noticed was that most of the credit doctors were not really local.

Most of the companies that advertised locally were from another part of the country. Not really a big deal as we are a global economy these days.

Here are some of the ads that came up local:

These ads were listed on a local website. They were very similar to the nationally advertised companies. The *outrageous guarantees* are what you may want to be aware of.

Some of the *guarantees* are unbelievable. Some say that they guarantee you a credit score of 720 within 30 days. Some guarantee they will remove all of your negative and derogatory reports. I'm not sure how some of these guarantees can be made.

I have helped many people with their credit for several years. My experience is that there is a pretty good chance your score can go up and also there is a fairly good chance that your score may go down. I'm not really sure that all of these credit doctors have your best interest at heart.

Another thing that I find fascinating is their *fees*. They all charge in different ways for different *services*. Some charge you a flat fee. Others charge you per *deletion* of derogatory information. Some charge you a combination of fees.

The fees are not what I have a problem with. I personally have a problem with what they do for you. Actually, I have a problem with what they *do not* do for *you*. They all seem to be pretty good at taking your money.

I have yet to see one *credit doctor* that can do *anything* for you that you cannot do yourself. You do not need to spend a lot of money with a credit doctor. You can improve your credit score and your financial situation with just a little education.

I will be revealing the best-kept secrets to improving your credit score in the last chapter. With a little basic education, you will know more than most of the credit doctors out there. Maybe you can teach them the *hidden secrets*.

What About Consumer Credit Counseling?

Looking up Consumer Credit Counseling Services this is what I found on Google:

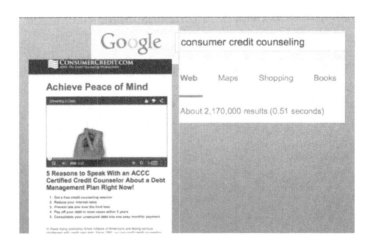

Consumer Credit Counseling Services were originally set up as nonprofit agencies to assist those that may need some counseling in regard to their finances and debt budgeting.

When I was a mortgage broker, we seen many that went through CCC. Their program can work good for many. Be aware of what may be going on with your credit in regard to the program.

There are many lenders that will not lend money to those on such programs. The credit reports can indicate that the *account is being handled by consumer credit counseling*. Many lenders will put this in the same category as a bankruptcy.

The program is a good match for many. They will consolidate your bills into one monthly payment. You will make your consolidated payment to the agency and they will in turn pay your creditors.

This is the same way that many credit repair doctors will consolidate you bills into one monthly payment. This can be good for some and there are some things you want to be aware of.

Many of these programs give you the impression that they will negotiate your accounts on your behalf. They may say that they will lower your payments, interest rates, remove late fees, etc.

There is not someone getting on the phone and negotiating your actual bills. It does sound good. Sounds like it's worth whatever it cost sometimes to avoid the creditor and let someone else help you. Not exactly how it works.

There is a list put out periodically that shows what all the creditors in the country will do if you are to enroll in such programs. Each creditor has their guidelines of what they will do with these programs.

Some companies will go to 0% interest rates. Some will drop the late fees. And still others will go to a low monthly payment regardless of the balance. Every company has a different way of dealing with these programs.

This can be a good way to deal with debts and to avoid bankruptcy. Just know what you are getting into. You may be getting yourself in a better payment situation and at the same time hurting your credit score. Be aware.

Should I Really be Concerned About Identity Theft?

Chapter 9: Should I Really be Concerned About Identity Theft?

Chapter 9

Should I Really be Concerned About Identity Theft?

As a young child my mother told me I could be anyone I want. As it turns out this is identity theft. ~**Unknown**~

Should I Really be Concerned About Identity Theft?

A better question might be, "How concerned should I be about identity theft?" Today is easier than ever to have your identity stolen. Thieves today do not have to go any farther than their computer to steal your identity.

The best defense against identity theft is to be proactive and do the best you can to prevent it *before* your identity is stolen. Is it best to pay a company to do this for me? Is identity theft prevention something I can do on my own?

Whether you pay a company that *may* be able to help you prevent identity theft or do it on your *own* or do *nothing* is a decision that you *will* make. If you do nothing, nothing will change.

We will look at a couple of different choices that you will have to decide. *Some people* choose to do something before there is a problem with their identity.

Some *other people* want to *pay* a company that may be able to help them. And still some of *those other* people simply choose to do nothing at all and remain vulnerable to identity thieves that are lurking out there.

First let's talk a look at *those other* people that choose to do nothing and some of the results they may get. Unfortunately, this has happened to many that were not knowledgeable of the threat. This may be you at this point.

Even if you have already been a victim of identity theft, you can prevent further damage. Once you know your options, you can help yourself and at the very least share them with others.

Is there anything I can do if my identity has already been stolen and someone else has used or abused my credit?

These can be very difficult situations to straighten out. Most creditors do not *care* if this happens to you. Many will not prosecute the perpetrators.

The amounts that are stolen through identity theft are simply not large enough for them to spend their time, money and resources on. And they won't go out of their way to help you, understandably.

The amounts of money usually stolen is kept under ten thousand dollars. This is the amount that is under the creditor *radar* limit they are not concerned with. The professional thieves seem to know this.

By the time you notice that a thief has tarnished your credit, they are usually done with you and have moved on. In just a couple of short months a criminal may be able to open several accounts in your name. They will most often change to their mailing address.

The sooner that you notice that your information has been compromised the better. There is not a lot of help out there once you have been violated.

The authorities including law enforcement are not always very helpful. The laws are not very severe and are difficult to enforce and prosecute. They have way more important things to tend to. This is not exactly terrorism. Or is it?

I personally have had my credit information breeched at least six times. My credit cards and personal bank account were jeopardized. I did not lose a dime.

There are ways to deal with this and be proactive. The first time I had a credit card stolen was at the airport as far as I could tell. Checking my bag in at the kiosk the attendant had difficulty running my *new* AMEX card with his reader.

He said, "I need to run your card inside. It'll only take a minute." I didn't think much about it. A couple of days later I received an email from American Express about some unusual activity on my account.

I called them and they asked if I had recently made a purchase at *Game Stop* or *Victoria's Secret*. I assured them I had not as I had been out of town on business in a different part of the country.

They canceled my card, changed the number and sent me a new one. No money lost out of my pocket. There was some inconvenience. We figured that it might have had something to do with the airport incidence. Especially since it was the first time the card was used.

Another time I was in San Diego at a conference. I just happen to be up about four in the morning as I was adjusted to a different time zone. When looking at my email there was an alert.

They wanted me to call ASAP. So, I did. After giving them my security information, they asked me if I was buying airline tickets in the Philippines. I assured them I was not buying tickets right then on that part of the globe.

My account was canceled, and I was issued a new card. There was no personal money lost by me. A new card was issued. Inconvenience was the loss again.

There was an incident not too long ago that was maybe a little more inconvenient. A couple of my friends were visiting us from Chicago. One afternoon we decided to go out for lunch.

We had a great lunch. Stayed for a while and had a nice visit. When it came time to leave, I went to pay the check. As I usually do, I gave our server my debit card.

The server came back and told me that my debit card was declined. She said they were having problems with their machine. No big deal. So, I gave her my credit card.

A few minutes later she came back and said that my credit card did not go through and was declined. Not wanting to do this again with another card I gave her cash.

When we got back to the condo, I logged on to my bank account. Everything seemed to be fine. There was plenty of money and nothing unusual. Didn't think much more about it.

My friends went back home. A few days later I was at a store to buy a few things. My bill was about twenty-eight dollars. After scanning my debit card, the cashier informed me that it was declined.

I paid cash at the store and rushed home. Logging on to my account I saw there was plenty of money and an urgent *alert*. Apparently, it took a little while for the alert to catch up with me.

After going through several channels of security and finally getting to the right *security guard* they explained what happened. Security told me that there was some very suspicious activity on my account.

They also told me that if they froze my accounts, they knew I would contact them. They were right. I did contact them. They also told me why they did not think it was me. It turned out to be very much appreciated.

I had used my debit card right before my friends from out of town had visited. It was at a small restaurant I had never been to before. Not completely putting the blame on them and at the same time I had not used it anywhere else for quite a while.

The bank security informed me that someone had opened up an account at a major home improvement supply center in Atlanta. They know I'm from St. Louis.

The main thing I was affected by was the inconvenience. I did not lose a dime. Am I lucky? Yes. I also can add some value in to being proactive on identity theft.

So what are My options to prevent Identity Theft?

What are the benefits of having a *company* take care of this for me? The companies out there seem to be advertising heavily. Identity theft seems to be very good *buzzwords* these days.

After all, who wants to have their identity stolen and deal with all the aftermath that comes with it? No one. Some *other people* and that may be you, choose to pay one of *those* companies to monitor this for them.

There are a few of those companies out there these days. Many choose to pay a fee to prevent identity theft. Makes sense, right? Seems to make sense.

The advertisements make it sound like when you *sign* up for their services, they will be watching your credit report, bank accounts, your back and your grandmothers' chickens. In reality you are signing up for an ongoing fee.

I Googled "identity theft" and this is what they came up with:

Google | identity theft

Web   News   Images   Videos   Books   More ▾   Search tools

About 105,000,000 results (0.29 seconds)

As you can see, they shared one hundred and five million results. This was in only point two nine seconds. That's a lot of results. Must be something to look at.

As I researched this identity theft, I attempted to see what you got for your *membership fee*. A major advertiser guarantees a $1,000,000 guarantee if someone steals your identity.

The company does say that no one can completely guarantee identity theft. This is true. They also say they may be able to help you if your identity is stolen.

As far as I could tell the one-million-dollar guarantee is an insurance policy. My thoughts are that I could *insure* a lot of people for identity theft as I'm collecting $30 to $60 + per month. Especially when I'm collecting from maybe 1 million or more per month. I wish I had thought of this.

Okay, I want to be proactive and prevent identity theft, and do it by myself?

It can be very simple to prevent identity theft *before* it happens and do it yourself. There are some simple steps you may take prevent being the *victim*.

One seemingly obvious thing that you can do defensively is to *not* give your personal information out to just anyone. Things such as your date of birth, social security number, home address, mother's maiden name, dog's name as well as other information should be shared cautiously.

When throwing out personal information in the trash with your social security, date of birth, account numbers, etc. it is best to shred them.

Although not as prevalent as it once was there are still *dumpster divers*. Dumpster divers are those that will sift through your trash for personal information that may be available to establish new accounts with *your* personal information.

 Be extremely cautious these days of fraudulent emails. Many appear to be *warnings* about your personal account. They may say your account is scheduled to be closed or suspended.

Many copy actual logos and other *official* looking things from real company websites. Most have a link that you can *conveniently* click onto so you can make the necessary corrections.

These are known as *phishing* emails. They are sent not really knowing if you have an account with the company or not. They try to alarm you so you will click onto the link and enter your login and password information. There are many other ways they attempt to get your information by email.

The best way to verify a real or a phishing email is to either call the company on their phone number or open up another web browser and log on there.

The international crooks have become more proficient lately. They have become very good and can be thousands of miles away. Many are from *Nigeria*. Apparently, the prosecution laws are pretty lax.

One of the simplest and quickest things you can do is to add a fraud statement to your credit report.

One of the simplest and quickest things you can do is to add a fraud statement to your credit report. You can actually add any statement to your credit report up to 100 words. We'll look at *any* statement later.

You'll need to send your fraud statement to all three of the credit bureaus. It is very easy to do and may save you years of anguish just by being a little proactive.

What should your statement say? Simple is always best. It needs to be very clear and right to the point. Simply put, it should include:

"Do not extend credit to anyone using my name and social security number without first obtaining a government issued picture ID and also calling me to confirm this on my personal phone line. The number that must be called is XXX-XXX-XXXX."

This very simple statement can keep someone from opening up new credit accounts in your name. It needs to be updated from time to time. Once a year should be sufficient.

This should prevent any new accounts being opened with your information that you do not authorize. It will not prevent your current accounts from being hacked into.

With most of your credit accounts there is a maximum liability of seventy-five dollars, to you, if someone does steal your account and then uses it.

As mentioned earlier, my information has been stolen a few times. I have not lost one dime. I have spent some time and a little aggravation getting it resolved. My credit was never in jeopardy.

How EASY is it to Dispute Information on MY Credit Report?

Chapter 10: How EASY is it to Dispute Information on MY Credit Report?

Chapter 10

How EASY is it to Dispute Information on MY Credit Report?

"Don't look at where you fall, but where you slipped." ~African Proverb~

How EASY is it to dispute information on MY credit report?

There is a lot of talk these days about removing negative things from your credit report. Many of *those* credit doctors will lead you to believe that they know some hidden *secret* that you cannot find out about.

The truth is, there is no *magic* that only *those* credit doctors know, when it comes to your credit report. There are just a few things that you may not know. At least, so far.

That's why you are reading this. With just a little education you will know as much and probably more than *those* credit doctors. Disputing negative information is very easy.

According to FCRA (Fair Credit Reporting Act) you may dispute *incorrect* information on your credit report. You may actually dispute *any* information on your credit report.

You must keep in mind that any time that you dispute information on your credit report you may just wake up a sleeping dog that could come back to haunt you.

There are no guarantees that information you dispute will be removed from your report. Even if a negative entry is getting aged it may remain and even make it worse for you and your score.

When entries are disputed, the creditor may confirm the information. Many times, they will update the information and make it worse.

I am amazed at all of *those credit doctors* that make those outlandish guarantees. I don't know how they can make some of the claims that they do. Many charge hundreds and even thousands of dollars for these *guarantees*.

My experience with disputed information on your credit report is that some information is removed, and some is not. Yes, there is a good chance that negative information may be removed. There is also a good chance that the negative information may not be removed.

How do you go about removing incorrect and/or negative information from your credit report?

To attempt to remove incorrect and/or negative information from your credit report, simply requires you to write a letter to the credit bureaus.

You will need to write to all three credit bureaus to ensure that there is a chance for removal. There are still no guarantees. So, what do you say?

Keep your words very simple and brief. I've included some sample letters in the last chapter. Your statement should say something like:

In regard to the *BuyNowNeverEverPay* payday loan, account number 1234567, it is incorrect. Please verify the information and remove when completed. Send me confirmation when done.

Whenever you dispute information on the credit report, the bureau must respond in a reasonable amount of time. There are few things that could transpire.

The bureau may do nothing if they think you are making a frivolous claim. They may also contact the creditor to verify the information. At this point there could be different outcomes.

The creditor may agree with you and report back to the credit bureau that you are right. There's really not a great chance of this happening.

The creditor may do nothing and not even respond to the dispute. This is pretty common. This is also what many of *those* credit doctors are counting on. Many of those *guarantees* they give you are counting on this.

What if a creditor confirms the negative dispute?

There is always a good chance that a creditor may confirm a negative disputed item. Information good and bad is supposed to stay on your credit report for seven years, ten years for bankruptcy.

There's a chance that a creditor will not only confirm the dispute, they may even update the information. This can have a terrible effect on your score.

When negative things are updated on your credit report there is a good chance that your score will drop. I have seen many instances where someone had attempted to remove a *collection* and when they updated it, the person's score went down.

Always keep in mind that there are *no guarantees* that you will be able to remove negative information form your credit report. You may have a good chance of removing information, just no guarantees.

You do not want to dispute anything on your credit report when you are applying for credit. You may wake up that sleeping dog and do more harm than good. Much more on this and other steps to improving your credit in the next chapter.

What if I Have NO Credit – Bad Credit or I am Starting from ZERO?

Chapter 11: What if I Have NO Credit – Bad Credit or I am Starting from ZERO?

Chapter 11

What if I Have NO Credit – Bad Credit or I am Starting from ZERO?

"Zero is the number people often feel more so than one." ~Anthony Liccione

What if you have No Credit or I am starting from ZERO?

Contrary to popular belief No debt is Not always good or in your best interest as far as your credit is concerned. Being *debt free* is not always beneficial.

There is such a thing called *credit utilization.* You need to show that you can use your credit responsibly. You must have open, positive accounts in today's world.

What if you already totally screwed up your credit and now need to start from Below ZERO?

Many of us have *life situations* that just seem to *happen* to us. We go through a lot of things today that our grandparents did not foresee. There are divorces, illnesses, accidents, job losses, disasters, deaths and lawsuits just to name a few of the things that we are susceptible to today.

There are many reasons that our credit may get totally *screwed* up. This is *restarting* or starting from *Below ZERO*. Many of us have been below zero and this maybe you. Don't worry. You can restart with an *almost* fresh start.

There are two types of revolving credit cards that are available. There are **unsecured** and **secured** credit cards. We'll look at both.

The **unsecured** credit cards are simply that. They are not secured by any collateral. The creditor will extend a pre-set amount of money to you based on your word. You promise to pay back the amount you borrow with interest.

On the other hand, **secured** credit cards can be a good tool when you are establishing or re-establishing credit. They are usually secured by funds or collateral that you put up with the creditor.

How do you start from ZERO or Below?

What if you have applied for an *unsecured* credit card and have been turned down? You may have applied to a few creditors with the same result. There may still be an alternative for you.

If you are unable to obtain an *unsecured* credit card you may be able to get a *secured* credit card. That is one that is secured with your own money. A good place to start is where you do your own personal banking.

Contact your bank or credit union and ask if they have a secured credit card available. The way this work is you will put up a portion of your own money, say $300 to $500, as collateral.

They will issue a Visa or Mastercard to you secured by your money. Sometimes these accounts are connected with your ATM accounts. This can be a great way to establish or reestablish your credit.

A very important factor is to make sure they report the secured account to all three credit bureaus. If they don't, the account may not do you much good. They must report your credit activities to start from zero or below.

What if they do *not* grant credit to you, even a secured account? There are other sources to come up from zero and below. We'll take a look at other ways.

There are several companies that will offer secured credit cards to those wanting to establish or re-establish credit. Some of these companies offer unsecured and secured accounts.

These companies charge very high interest rates and they come with steep fees. They might issue you an account with a $300 limit and immediately charge you fees of $180 at 28.9% interest.

That's quite a high cost for what seems to be a little credit. Is it really a *little* credit? This can be a good resource when you are coming up from zero or below. The cost may actually be low in many instances.

With a balance, limit and cost you will want to pay off the amount as soon as possible. You will start off with too high of a balance to limit ratio. We explore more details on balance to limit percentages in the last chapter.

Since it takes six months of reporting for the score to develop or redevelop, you'll want to utilize your account each month. Buy something you were going to buy anyway such as a tank of gas. Pay the statement balance in full each month. Six months will go by quickly.

Make sure they will report the account to all three bureaus. Even though many of these companies will charge very high interest rates and fees remember, you are working on improving your credit score.

As your score improves so will your choices for better rate and fee credit cards. Sometimes it's worth a little extra money to improve your situation.

What if you are so far below ZERO no one will even issue you a secured credit card?

You may still have another alternative. One way is to become an authorized user on someone else's account. A relative or someone close to you may want to help you gain or re-gain credit.

One way that many establish and reestablish credit is that they are added as an authorized user on one or more of someone else's established accounts.

This will allow the history of their credit account to be reported on your credit report also. Do not abuse this opportunity. Not only will you be hurting yourself, but you will also be hurting that person's credit.

If you are the relative helping someone by letting them use your credit, I would recommend not giving the person you are helping the credit card itself. Keep in mind that this is your credit at risk, and you do not want a seven-year mistake.

7 Simple Steps to a Higher Credit Score

&

Avoiding a Debt Sentence

Chapter 12: 7 Simple Steps to a Higher Credit Score & Avoiding a Debt Sentence

Chapter 12

7 Simple Steps to a Higher Credit Score

&

Avoiding a Debt Sentence

"No man with a complex life can be happy! The simple secret of happiness is a simple life." ~Mehmet Murat ildan~

What can **I** *do to* **Increase** *My credit score?*

There are a few things that you can do to increase your credit score to a *stellar* status. Most of these things are just common sense. By taking these steps you just may have more common sense than *those* credit doctors.

When simplifying the ways to improve your credit score, I broke it down into *7 simple* steps. These are very easy things that you can do on your own *without* one of *those* credit doctors.

Just by following these simple steps you can save thousands and thousands of dollars. Keep in mind that there are no guarantees. Anytime you attempt to improve your credit score you may actually decrease you score. How could this happen?

Many times, when you are disputing negative information on your credit report it will have a negative effect. There is a good chance that an old collection or derogatory account will be updated.

Collection information, whether paid off or not, could be updated by the collection company. Your score does not calculate the difference in a collection that has been paid off and one that is still owed. It has to do with how recently the collection has been reported.

According to FCRA, information remains on your credit report for seven years. It does not matter if it is negative or positive. Bankruptcies remain for ten years. As mentioned earlier they may not always have a long-term negative effect depending on some other factors.

When is the Best time to work on improving your credit?

The best time to work on improving your credit report is when you are *not* applying for credit. As previously mentioned, you may be waking up a sleeping dog. This sleeping dog could be the difference in getting approved for credit or not.

There are times, you are not even aware of negative and derogatory things on your credit report until you apply for something. By attempting to resolve or remove something you could actually make your situation worse.

By getting a copy of your credit report on a regular basis you may be able to avoid unwanted surprises when applying for credit. A lot of people get these unwanted surprises when they could have avoided them.

What are the 7 simple steps to improving your score and avoiding a *debt sentence?*

7 Simple Steps to Improving Your Credit
Score:

1) *Pay* Your Bills – On Time

2) *Don't* necessarily close older and/or paid off accounts

3) *Don't* get unnecessary credit inquiries

4) *Keep* balance in proportion to credit limits at 30-40% or less on revolving accounts

5) *Dispute* incorrect information

6) *Add* a fraud and/or any statement to your credit report

7) Smile, Relax & Sleep well tonight

1) Pay Your Bills – On Time

This may seem pretty obvious. The first place to start is to pay your bills and your obligations. And pay them *on time*. All of your bills have a due date. If you do not pay by the due date many will charge you a late fee.

Many credit accounts such a credit cards and revolving accounts will charge you a late fee if your account is not credited by the due date. Most of these, charge you a flat fee.

Most credit card companies these days will also raise your interest rate if you are late three times within the year. According to most *user agreements* they may raise your interest rate based your payment history with other creditors.

There are many companies today that offer to *give* you your *FICO* score each month as a *courtesy* to you. Just be aware that they are looking at your credit report each month. If there is something they don't like, they may change the account they have with you.

These are *soft* credit inquiries. We'll get into this a little more in a bit. This is just one of the ways you may be adversely affected by a creditor.

What about accounts like mortgages? Some companies give you a *grace* period each month. You may have a due date of the first of the month and they will not charge you a late fee until the fifteenth. First of all, you must understand that this *grace* period does not come from the *credit angels*. They may not be charging you a late fee, and they are charging you interest. Interest is calculated on the outstanding balance and will be used in your pay off.

Since your payment history accounts for thirty percent of your credit score the impact it has is huge. Payments made and payments made on time are just common sense.

2) **Don't** *necessarily close older and/or paid off accounts*

Many of *those* credit doctors will tell you to close some of your accounts. This is not always in your best interest. It may seem like good advice to close an old account. It may seem like a good idea to close a paid off account.

If you have had a sketchy payment history on an account, it may seem like a good idea to close the account and cut ties with that account. Don't be too quick to close those accounts.

The length of your credit history accounts for fifteen percent of your overall credit score. By closing accounts that you have had for a while, you may be shortening your credit history and adversely affect your score.

Just because you have a not-so-perfect payment history with a creditor does not mean you should close the account. Closing the account will not erase your payment history.

The more time that goes by from late payments the less it will affect your credit score. Time can be one of the greatest factors when working on increasing your score.

It may be in your best interest to stop using an account. You may want to think twice before closing an account. Fifteen percent may not seem like a big percentage. It may be the difference in several percent points on a thirty-year mortgage.

3) Don't *get unnecessary credit inquiries*

There are two types of credit inquiries. There are *hard* and *soft* credit inquiries. What is the difference in hard and soft credit inquiries? Let's take a look.

A hard credit inquiry is when you apply for credit and give permission for the potential creditor to pull and view a copy of your credit report.

Hard credit inquiries stay on your credit report for two years. If you have a lot of recent credit inquiries it will have a negative effect on your score. The more time that elapses from the inquiries the less impact it will have on your score.

The exceptions to having many credit inquiries affect your score is inquiries from shopping for a mortgage or an automobile. The credit bureaus give you a *window* of time when shopping.

During this window of time each inquiry will not be counted separately. They will be grouped together. On the other hand, if you are shopping for cars every week on your day off and they are pulling hard copies of your credit report it will count against you.

The other types of credit inquiries are soft inquiries. Soft inquiries do not count toward your credit score. They do show up on your report and you can see who has been looking at you.

A soft inquiry is an authorization that you give to a creditor that lets them look at your credit report whenever they choose to. This authorization is usually spelled out in the fine print of their *user agreement*.

How many times have you actually read the user agreement of your credit accounts? Most of us have never looked at the user agreement little alone read it. We give our creditors a lot more freedom than then we may know.

Many companies are acting like they are doing you a favor by *giving* you your FICO score with your bill each month. Are they really doing you a favor?

Maybe they just want to see how you are paying your accounts. Maybe they are looking for reasons that my lead to changing the terms to your account. Maybe they are looking for reasons to raise your rates and fees. I don't know. Be aware.

Overall credit inquiries account for ten percent of our credit scores. Ten percent may not seem like a big factor or concern. Ten percent may be the difference in a 700-credit score and a 630-credit score.

Ten percent could make the difference in who chooses to do business with you. It can make the difference of who *you* choose to do business with. Ten percent can make a very big difference in the rate that the creditor will charge you. This can be thousands and thousands of dollars.

Besides not shopping for things such as cars all the time there are also some other things you can do to avoid unnecessary credit inquiries.

Don't sign up for the credit card at the football-tailgating booth simply to get the stadium blanket. This will be a hard inquiry. You may also want to think twice before signing up for the store credit card to get a 10% discount today. More on this next, with proportion to limits.

4) Keep *balances in proportion to limits at 30-40% or less on revolving accounts*

The proportion of balance to limits is one of the biggest factors that affect our credit scores. This is probably one of the least understood factors. Many of *those* credit doctors say that it is the total amount that you owe.

The total amount you owe has nothing to do with your credit score. Credit scores are calculated not on the amount that you owe but rather on proportion of balances to limits on your revolving accounts.

Revolving accounts are accounts such as credit cards, store cards and payday loans. The dollar amounts do not matter. The percentages do matter.

Based on percentages a person that has a five thousand with a four-thousand-dollar balance will score lower than someone with a balance of two hundred thousand dollars and a one-million-dollar limit.

What about store specific credit cards that are only accepted at those stores? I personally do not carry or own any store cards. Major credit cards are accepted at just about every store. I do not see a need for me to have one.

Typically store cards tend to have lower limits on them. The balances also seem to be higher in proportion to the limits. They were not created to have large limits. They were created to get you to buy something now.

Many retail stores these days will offer you a discount of maybe ten percent off of the purchase today, when you apply and open a credit account with them.

You may be thinking, why not open an account so I can get a discount now? I'm going to buy this item anyway. Not so fast. You may want to look at the consequences.

As stated before, you will more than likely receive a hard credit inquiry. This may adversely affect your overall credit score as we learned before. The other factor that you need to be aware of is the proportion of the balance to the limit they will give you.

You may be purchasing a four-hundred-dollar item. The clerk might offer you a credit account that will instantly give you ten percent off of the item. At first it may sound pretty good.

You might think today, I'm getting a four-hundred-dollar item for only three hundred and sixty dollars. I was going to buy it anyway. My credit is pretty good so what can it hurt?

What it could hurt is your credit score. They may open up an account for your three hundred sixty-dollar item with a five-hundred-dollar limit. This will instantly put you at seventy two percent balance to limit ratio!

This can really make a difference on your credit score if it's your only account. The total credit accounts collectively are calculated and not just the new store card.

Overall you may have a total limit of available credit at maybe twenty thousand dollars. With one five-thousand-dollar account that is maxed out it will be considered with all of your limits. In this example you would be at twenty five percent, which is well within the guidelines.

Keeping your proportion in regard to your limits in line can be one of the biggest factors affecting your credit score. This can also be another reason you not close your older accounts. Your total limits can be affected tremendously.

5) *Dispute incorrect information*

In the last chapter we talked about disputing negative information on our credit reports. According to FCRA you can dispute incorrect information that is on your credit report.

The disputed information must be investigated by the credit bureau *unless* they deem the request as fraudulent. The bureaus are required to get in touch with the creditor that has reported the derogatory information. The must do this in a timely manner and report the findings back to you.

This can take a while and does not always turn out with the results you were hoping for. There is always the chance that the creditor will update the information reporting *new* negative information.

There is always the possibility that the creditor will not respond. They may not use their resources, i.e. their time and money, to update your account. If they do not confirm your account, it will more than likely be removed.

A lot of *those* credit doctors depend on and *guarantee* they can remove this derogatory information and improve your credit score. My experience is that the on guarantee is something may change.

There is a good chance that a derogatory account will be removed simply from disputing it. There is also a good chance that you will be waking up a sleeping dog that may cause you more problems.

Many new credit accounts you may be applying for, such as a mortgage, may require you to pay off older collections and accounts. This could be okay if you do not need to worry about your credit score such as with an FHA mortgage.

When you are required to deal with older accounts you may want to choose an alternative way to deal with them. If you are required to pay off an older collection you may want to see if you can pay it at the time of loan closing.

If the creditor insists that the account be paid ahead of your loan closing, you may still use this to your advantage. If you must contact the creditor and pay them off, ask if you pay them will they remove this from your credit report completely.

Many collection accounts, particularly older accounts, are willing to work with you in some respects. If they agree to remove the derogatory information from your credit report by you paying it, get this agreement in writing. Get them to put it on their letterhead.

Check with the credit bureau after the account is paid off and make sure they followed up with their end of the bargain. Another thing that may help you when you are paying off old debts is to negotiate the payoff amount.

Why would a collector negotiate with you? One reason that creditors will negotiate the payoff amount is simply that they would rather get some of their money than what they have been getting which is usually zero.

The amount that they may be currently reporting to the credit bureau may be more than just the defaulted balance. Many times, it may include several fees such as late fees, accumulated interest and legal fees. There may very well be some *wiggle* room for negotiating.

A lot of times it may be in your best interest to let someone else negotiate on your behalf. Most of us can become emotional when we are dealing with our own negative accounts.

A lot of this emotion can stem from the fact that it may bring up a lot of bad sentiment from the past. These accounts may be from an old medical bill that reminds us a bad illness when we had no insurance.

It may also bring up some past bills that were the result from a bad divorce we may have gone through. I have to say that I cannot recall anyone ever telling me about a *good* divorce that they went through.

There can be a lot of other emotions that are brought forward by bringing up the negative past. By letting a third party negotiate for you may be able to leave much of it in the past.

6) Add *a fraud and/or any statement to your credit report*

In the last chapter we talked about adding a fraud statement to your credit report. This will *not* help to raise your credit score. It will help to prevent someone from using your information to establish credit for them without your consent.

You can add any statement to your credit report up to one hundred words. This can be very helpful in explaining your situation. It will not necessarily improve your credit score. It will *not* hurt your credit score.

There are many reasons that you may want to add a statement to your credit report. You may have had an illness that required medical treatment and had no insurance. You may have lost a job and become delinquent on some of your accounts.

In my own personal situation, I went through a not-so-good divorce. I became late on many of my bills. Eventually I did pay all of my bills and brought everything current.

Many years later I was applying for a new mortgage and my negative credit became something of interest. Not so much a care for me as the loan company, or so I thought. As it turned out it was a care for me.

There were many things from the past that I had to deal with. It did not and does not just simply *go away*. This was very time consuming and took several months to get things the way the creditor wanted it.

At the time I had a regular full-time job. It was almost like taking on a part-time job getting my credit back in line. I discovered much about how and why credit works. My experience can save you much heartache, especially time and money.

One of the *secrets* that I came across was the prevision that lets you add a statement to your credit report, in your own words of up to 100 words. I thought," This is great!" I can explain my situation.

Finally, everyone will know that I'm really not a deadbeat. I'm just a regular person like everyone else that went through a difficult time. I couldn't wait to get started.

I thought out my statement very carefully. Working on it for several days I wanted to get all of my facts down and I could do state this in my *own words*.

One of the things that I found out with this process is that the credit bureau can actually *edit* your statement. I worked very diligently on my statement and thought that I did a pretty good job. Being very proud I had my statement down to 99 words and choosing my verbiage very carefully.

For some reason whoever decided to edit my statement, took out the part about me being divorced from a devastating witch. I thought that was an important part of my story. I was careful not to use too colorful or saucy words, or at least I thought.

After the edit my added statement was down to 94 words. It still explained most of story, just not with details I had written.

What kinds of statements are you allowed to add to your credit report? Let's look at some examples of what may be added to your credit report.

Samples of what you may be able to add to your credit report (more details in the workbook section):

April 15, 2015

To Whom It May Concern:

There is some incorrect information on my credit report that needs to be verified and corrected.

J.J. Pennry account number 345987 is not my account and I do not owe them any money. Please verify this information and delete the account when updated. Let me know when the correction has been made.

Thank you.

John Q. Doe
SSN 555-55-5555

123 Main Street
Anytown USA 11111

April 15, 2015

To Whom It May Concern:

The following is a consumer statement that I would like to be added to my credit report:

In regards to the late payments that are reporting on my credit report from July 2012 and December 2012, they were due to an accident I suffered at work. During this time I was delinquent due to my injury. Since than I have returned to work and have caught up on all of my obligations.

Thank you.

John Q. Doe
SSN 555-55-5555

123 Main Street
Anytown USA 11111

April 15, 2015

To Whom It May Concern:

Due to Identity theft concerns please add the following Fraud Statement to my credit report:

Do Not extent credit to anyone using my name and social security number without first obtaining a government issued picture I.D. and calling me on my personal phone for further verification. You may call me @ 123-555-3245.

Thank you.

John Q. Doe
SSN 555-55-5555

123 Main Street

Send your statements to:

The Three Major Credit Reporting Bureaus:

Experian

701 Experian Parkway
P.O. Box 4500
Allen TX 75013*
1.888.397.3742

Trans Union

2 Baldwin Place
P.O. Box 1000
Chester PA 19022 *
1.800.916.8800

Equifax

P.O. Box 740256
Atlanta, GA 30374*
1.800.685.1111

*These addresses and phone numbers are current as of
publication. They do change from time to time. It is
recommended you verify the information before corresponding.

7) *Smile, Relax & Sleep well tonight*

With just a little education your credit score can go up by leaps and bounds. You have just learned in these few pages what has taken me twenty-five years to learn.

By getting your credit in order many other areas of your life will improve along with it. It is much easier to keep your credit in good shape once you get it under control.

The *secrets* you have just learned are what keep *those* credit doctors in business. There really are no secrets. There are just things you may not know yet. All of the information is out there and is not really a *secret*.

Share the knowledge you have accumulated with others. The more you help others the more you will get in return. I truly believe that everything should be shared for the common good of us all.

Dreams do come true. Expect more. Give more. Be more. Do more. Receive more.

Where Do I Start?

Chapter 13: Where Do I Start? - Workbook

Chapter 13
Where Do I Start? - Workbook

"The Secret to getting ahead is getting started." ~Mark Twain"

The first step in determining how to improve your credit score is to start where you are at right now. How do you do this?

Get a copy of your credit report. Where?

A good place to get a *Free* snapshot of your credit report with the score is CreditKarma.com

Score_____   Date_____

Score_____   Date_____

Score_____   Date_____

Score_____   Date_____

Score_____   Date_____

Score_____   Date_____

Score_____   Date_____

Score_____   Date_____

Score_____   Date_____

Score_____   Date_____

Score_____   Date_____

Score_____   Date_____

How Are Scores Calculated?

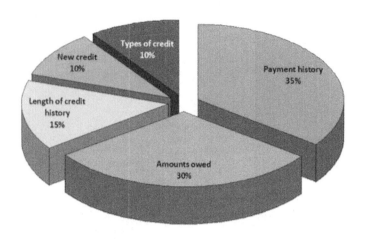

- **35% = Payment History**

- **10% = Types of Credit**

- **10% = Credit Inquiries**

- **15% = Credit History**

- **30% = Amount, i.e. Proportion of Balance to Limits**

Payment History/How Paid = 35%

Account_____Paid__On Time
---30 Days Late---60 DL---90 DL

Account_____Paid__OT__30__60__90

Account_____Paid__OT__30__60__90

Account_____Paid__OT__30__60__90

Account_____Paid__OT__30__60__90

Account_____Paid__OT__30__60__90

Account_____Paid__OT__30__60__90

Account_____Paid__OT__30__60__90

Account_____Paid__OT__30__60__90

Account_____Paid__OT__30__60__90

Account_____Paid__OT__30__60__90

Types Of Accounts = 10%

**Account_____Revolving(CC)__Mortgage__
Auto__StoreCard__PayDayLoan__Other**

Account_____CC__Mort__A__SC__PDL__O

Account_____CC__Mort__A__SC__PDL__O

Account_____CC__Mort__A__SC__PDL__O

Account_____CC__Mort__A__SC__PDL__O

Account_____CC__Mort__A__SC__PDL__O

Account_____CC__Mort__A__SC__PDL__O

Account_____CC__Mort__A__SC__PDL__O

Account_____CC__Mort__A__SC__PDL__O

Account_____CC__Mort__A__SC__PDL__O

Account_____CC__Mort__A__SC__PDL__O

Credit Inquiries = 10%

of Inquiries

Last 6 months____

Last 12 months____

Last 24 months____

Credit History/Age of Accounts = 15%

Account_____Date Opened_____Age__

Account_____Date Opened_____Age____

Account_____Date Opened_____Age____

Account_____Date Opened_____Age____

Account_____Date Opened_____Age____

Account_____Date Opened_____Age____

Account_____Date Opened_____Age____

Account_____Date Opened_____Age____

Account_____Date Opened_____Age____

Account_____Date Opened_____Age____

Account_____Date Opened_____Age____

Amount Owed/Proportion of Balance to Limits = 30%

Account_____Balance_____
Credit Limit_____%_____

Account_____Balance_____
    Credit Limit_____%_____

Account_____Balance_____
    Credit Limit_____%_____

Account_____Balance_____
    Credit Limit_____%_____

Account_____Balance_____
    Credit Limit_____%_____

Account_____Balance_____
    Credit Limit_____%_____

Account_____Balance_____
    Credit Limit_____%_____

Account_____Balance_____
    Credit Limit_____%_____

Account_____Balance_____
    Credit Limit_____%_____

Account_____Balance_____
    Credit Limit_____%_____

Bankrupt Date Filed_____Chapter 11/13

Judgments Date Reported_____Type_____

Collections Date Reported_____Type____

Write dispute letters to the credit bureaus

Letters written_____Date Sent_____
Response Received____

Letters written_____Date Sent_____
Response Received____

Letters written_____Date Sent_____
Response Received____

Sample Dispute Letters

Sample Dispute Letter to Credit Bureaus

April 15, 2021

To Whom It May Concern:

There is some incorrect information on my credit report that needs to be verified and corrected.

J.J. Pennry account number 345987 is not my account and I do not owe them any money. Please verify this information and delete the account when updated. Let me know when the correction has been made.

Thank you.

John Q. Doe
SSN 555-55-5555

123 Main Street
Anytown USA 11111

Don't forget to sign it

Add a Fraud and/or Any Statement

Sample Fraud Statement to Add to Your Credit Report

April 15, 2021

To Whom It May Concern:

Due to Identity theft concerns please add the following Fraud Statement to my credit report:

Do Not extent credit to anyone using my name and social security number without first obtaining a government issued picture I.D. and calling me on my personal phone for further verification. You must also call me @ 123-555-3245.

Thank you.

John Q. Doe
SSN 555-55-5555

123 Main Street
Anytown USA 11111

Don't forget to sign it

Add a 100 word or less statement explaining your credit

Sample Explanation Statement

April 15, 2021

To Whom It May Concern:

Due to my current credit status, please add the following Credit explanation Statement to my credit report:

I recently went through a devastating divorce which caused me to pay some of my bills after the due dates. I also had an injury at work and did not have any income for a while. It added additional medical bills that were not covered by insurance. You must also call me @ 123-555-3245.

Thank you.

John Q. Doe
SSN 555-55-5555

123 Main Street
Anytown USA 11111

Don't forget to sign it

Three Major Credit Reporting Bureaus

Experian

701 Experian Parkway
P.O. Box 4500
Allen TX 75013

https://www.experian.com/consumer/upload//

1.888.397.3742

Trans Union

2 Baldwin Place
P.O. Box 1000
Chester PA 19022

https://dispute.transunion.com/dp/dispute/landingPage.jsp

1.800.916.8800

Equifax

P.O. Box 740256
Atlanta, GA 30374

https://www.ai.equifax.com/CreditInvestigation/
home.action

1.800.685.1111

*These addresses and phone numbers are current as of
publication. They do change from time to time. It is
recommended you verify the information before corresponding.

ID Theft and Tax-Return Fraud Concerns

Request Form 14039 from the IRS

Form **14039** Rev. February 2014	Department of the Treasury - Internal Revenue Service **Identity Theft Affidavit**	**OMB Number** 1545-2139

Complete and submit this form if you are an actual or potential victim of identity theft and would like the IRS to mark your account to identify questionable activity.

Check only one of the following two boxes if they apply to your specific situation. (Optional for all filers)

☐ I am submitting this form in response to a mailed notice or letter from the IRS.

☐ I am completing this form on behalf of another person, such as a deceased spouse or other deceased relative. You should provide information for the actual or potential victim in Sections A, B, & D.

Note to all filers: Failure to provide required information on **BOTH** sides of this form **AND** clear and legible documentation will delay processing.

THIS FORM MUST BE SIGNED ON THE REVERSE SIDE (SECTION F).

Section A – Reason For Filing This Form (Required for all filers)

Check only **ONE** of the following two boxes. You **MUST** provide the requested description or explanation in the lined area below.

1 ☐ I am a victim of identity theft **AND** it is affecting my federal tax records.

You should check this box if, for example, your attempt to file electronically was rejected because someone had already filed using your Social Security Number (SSN) or Individual Taxpayer Identification Number (ITIN), or if you received a notice or correspondence from the IRS indicating someone was otherwise using your number.

Provide a short explanation of the problem and how you were made aware of it.

2 ☐ I have experienced an event involving my personal information that may at some future time affect my federal tax records.

You should check this box if you are the victim of non-federal tax related identity theft, such as the misuse of your personal identity information to obtain credit. You should also check this box if no identity theft violation has occurred, but you have experienced an event that could result in identity theft, such as a lost/stolen purse or wallet, home robbery, etc.

Briefly describe the identity theft violation(s) and/or the event(s) of concern. Include the date(s) of the incident(s).

Section B – Taxpayer Information (Required for all filers)

Taxpayer's last name	First name	Middle initial	The last 4 digits of the taxpayer's SSN **or** the taxpayer's **complete** Individual Taxpayer Identification Number (ITIN)

Taxpayer's **current** mailing address (apt., suite no. and street, or P.O. Box)

City		State	ZIP code

Tax year(s) affected *(Required if you checked box 1 in Section A above)*	Last tax return filed (year) *(If you are not required to file a return, enter NRF and do not complete the next two lines)*

Address on last tax return filed *(If same as current address, write "same as above")*

City (on last tax return filed)	State	ZIP code

Section C – Telephone Contact Information (Required for all filers)

Telephone number *(Include area code)* ☐ Home ☐ Work ☐ Cell Best time(s) to call

I prefer to be contacted in *(select the appropriate language)* ☐ English ☐ Spanish ☐ Other

Section D – Required Documentation (Required for all filers)

Submit this completed form and a **clear and legible** photocopy of at least one of the following documents to verify your identity. If you are submitting this form on behalf of another person, the documentation should be for that person. If necessary, enlarge the photocopies so all information and pictures are clearly visible.

Check the box next to the document(s) you are submitting:

☐ Passport ☐ Driver's license ☐ Social Security Card ☐ Other valid U.S. Federal or State government issued identification**

** Do not submit photocopies of federally issued identification where prohibited by 18 U.S.C. 701 (e.g., official badges designating federal employment).

Form **14039** (Rev. 2-2014) Catalog Number 52525A www.irs.gov Department of the Treasury - Internal Revenue Service

Form 14039 Rev. February 2014	Department of the Treasury - Internal Revenue Service **Identity Theft Affidavit**	OMB Number 1545-2139

Section E – Representative Information (Required only if completing this form on someone else's behalf)

If you are completing this form on behalf of another person, you **must** complete this section **and attach clear and legible** photocopies of the documentation indicated.

Check only ONE of the following four boxes next to the reason why you are submitting this form

☐ The taxpayer is deceased and I am the surviving spouse. *(No attachments are required)*

☐ The taxpayer is deceased and I am the court-appointed or certified personal representative. Attach a copy of the court certificate showing your appointment.

☐ The taxpayer is deceased and a court-appointed or certified personal representative has not been appointed. Attach a copy of the death certificate or the formal notification from the appropriate government office informing the next of kin of the decedent's death. Indicate your relationship to the decedent: _____

☐ The taxpayer is unable to complete this form and I have been appointed conservator or have Power of Attorney (POA) authorization. Attach a copy of the documentation showing your appointment as conservator or your POA authorization. If you are the POA and have been issued a CAF number by the IRS, enter it here: _____

Representative's name

Current mailing address

City	State	ZIP code

Section F – Penalty Of Perjury Statement and Signature (Required for all filers)

Under penalty of perjury, I declare that, to the best of my knowledge and belief, the information entered on this form is true, correct, complete, and made in good faith.

Signature of taxpayer or representative of taxpayer	Date signed

Instructions for Submitting this Form

Submit this form and **clear and legible** copies of required documentation using **ONE** of the following submission options. Mailing **AND** faxing this form **WILL** result in a processing delay.

By Mail	By FAX
If you checked Box 1 in Section A and are unable to file your return electronically because the primary and/or secondary SSN was misused, attach this form and documentation to your paper return and submit to the IRS location where you normally file. **If you have already filed your paper return**, submit this form and documentation to the IRS location where you normally file. Refer to the "Where Do You File" section of your return instructions or visit IRS.gov and input the search term "Where to File."	If you checked Box 1 in Section A and are submitting this form in response to a notice or letter received from the IRS that shows a reply FAX number, FAX this completed form and documentation with a copy of the notice or letter to that number. Include a cover sheet marked "Confidential." If no FAX number is shown, follow the mailing instructions on the notice or letter.
If you checked Box 1 in Section A and are submitting this form in response to a notice or letter received from the IRS, return this form and documentation with a copy of the notice or letter to the address contained in the notice or letter. If you checked Box 2 in Section A (you do not currently have a tax-related issue), mail this form and documentation to: **Internal Revenue Service** PO Box 9039 Andover MA 01810-0939	If you checked Box 2 in Section A (you do not currently have a tax-related issue), FAX this form and documentation to: (855) 807-5720. NOTE: The IRS does not initiate contact with taxpayers by email, fax, or any social media tools to request personal or financial information. Report unsolicited email claiming to be from the IRS and bogus IRS websites to phishing@irs.gov. NOTE: For more information about questionable communications purportedly from the IRS, visit IRS.gov and input the search term "Fake IRS Communications".

Other helpful identity theft information may be found on www.irs.gov/uac/Identity-Protection. Additionally, locations and hours of operation for Taxpayer Assistance Centers can be found at www.irs.gov (search "Local Contacts").

Note: The Federal Trade Commission (FTC) is the central federal government agency responsible for identity theft awareness. The IRS does not share taxpayer information with the FTC. Refer to the FTC's website at www.identitytheft.gov for additional information, protection strategies, and resources.

Privacy Act and Paperwork Reduction Notice

Our legal authority to request the information is 26 U.S.C. 6001.

The primary purpose of the form is to provide a method of reporting identity theft issues to the IRS so that the IRS may document situations where individuals are or may be victims of identity theft. Additional purposes include the use in the determination of proper tax liability and to increase taxpayer burden. The information may be disclosed only as provided by 26 U.S.C. 6103. Providing the information on this form is voluntary. However, if you do not provide the information it may be more difficult to assist you in resolving your identity theft issue. If you are a potential victim of identity theft and do not provide the required substantiation information, we may not be able to place a marker on your account to assist with future protection. If you are a victim of identity theft and do not provide the required information, it may be difficult for IRS to determine your correct tax liability. If you intentionally provide false information, you may be subject to criminal penalties.

You are not required to provide the information requested on a form that is subject to the Paperwork Reduction Act unless the form displays a valid OMB control number. Books or records relating to a form or its instructions must be retained as long as their contents may become material in the administration of any Internal Revenue law. Generally, tax returns and return information are confidential, as required by section 6103.

Public reporting burden for this collection of information is estimated to average 15 minutes per response, including the time for reviewing instructions, searching existing data sources, gathering and maintaining the data needed, and completing and reviewing the collection of information. If you have comments concerning the accuracy of these time estimates or suggestions for making this form simpler, we would be happy to hear from you. You can write to the Internal Revenue Service, Tax Products Coordinating Committee, SE:W:CAR:MP:T:T:SP, 1111 Constitution Ave. NW, IR-6526, Washington, DC 20224. Do not send this form to this address. Instead, see the form for filing instructions. Notwithstanding any other provision of the law, no person is required to respond to, nor shall any person be subject to a penalty for failure to comply with, a collection of information subject to the requirements of the Paperwork Reduction Act, unless that collection of information displays a currently valid OMB Control Number.

Form **14039** (Rev. 2-2014)   Catalog Number 52525A   www.irs.gov   Department of the Treasury - Internal Revenue Service

Or go to:

http://www.irs.gov/uac/Tax-Fraud-Alerts

Secured Credit Card sources starting from ZERO & Below

Progress Credit – offers 3 mastercards

https://www.progresscredit.com/card_options

Open Sky – offers visa card

https://www.openskycc.com

OneUnited Bank – offers visa card

https://www.oneunited.com

First Choice Bank – offers 2 visa cards

http://www.securedcardchoice.com

Merrick Bank – offers visa card

https://securedcard.merrickbank.com

USAA Secured Cards – offers mastercard & American express card for US veterans

https://www.usaa.com/inet/pages/ banking_credit_cards_main? wa_ref=lf_product_bank_cc

Bad Credit – No Credit – Starting from ZERO & Below

Account applied for__Date__Response Recv'd___

Unsecured Cards

Acc_____Date_____Rcv'd_____

Acc_____Date_____Rcv'd_____

Acc_____Date_____Rcv'd_____

Secured Cards

Acc_____Date_____Rcv'd_____

Acc_____Date_____Rcv'd_____

Acc_____Date_____Rcv'd_____

Authorized User Accounts

Acc_____Date_____Rcv'd_____

Acc_____Date_____Rcv'd_____

Acc_____Date_____Rcv'd_____

7 Simple **Steps to Higher Credit Score**

&

Avoiding a *Debt Sentence*

1) Pay Your Bills – On Time

2) *Don't* necessarily close older and/or paid off accounts

3) *Don't* get unnecessary inquiries

4) *Keep* Balance in Proportion to Limits at 30-40% or less

5) *Dispute* Incorrect information

6) *A*dd a fraud and/or any statement to your credit report

7) *Smile*, Relax & Sleep well tonight

Glossary

Annual percentage rate (APR) – the effective rate of interest for a loan per year

Arrears – the amount of debt that is overdue or unpaid; a payment that is made past its due date

Asset – anything of value that can be converted into cash or used to pay a debt

Beacon Score/Pinnacle Score - A number generated by the Equifax Credit Bureau to rank an individual's creditworthiness.

Collateral – assets that are pledged by a borrower to secure a loan or other credit and that are subject to seizure in the event of default

Contract – a binding agreement between competent parties; to have a valid contract for sale of property, there must be 1) an offer, 2) an acceptance, 3) competent parties, 4) consideration, 5) legal purpose, 6) written documentation, 7) a description of the property and 8) signatures by principals or their attorney-in-fact

Courthouse – a building that is home to a local court of law and often the regional county government as well

Default – failure to meet legal obligations in a contract such as not making the agreed-upon monthly payments

Disclosure – statement of fact(s) concerning the condition of a property for that is up for sale

Empirica Score - The credit rating agency TransUnion uses a credit score called an Empirica score to rate people's credit.

Equifax – One of the three major credit bureaus.

Experian – One of the three major credit bureaus.

FICO Score – FICO is an acronym for the Fair Isaac Corporation, the creators of the FICO score used with Experian.

Due Diligence – 1) an investigation or audit of a potential investment that serves to confirm all material facts in regard to a sale; 2) the care a reasonable person should take before entering into an agreement or a transaction with another party

Grace Period – the time period between the date a payment is due and the date on which late charges will be assessed, for example, payments due on the 1st day of the month may have a 14 day grace period, meaning that fees will be charged if payment is not received by the 15th

Interest Rate – the percentage rate at which a principle amount will charged by a lender for the use of the funds

Lien – a claim against a property and/or person(s) for the purpose of collecting unpaid debts, judgments, mortgage payments or taxes

Mortgage – a written legal agreement that creates a lien against a property as security for the payment of a debt; a loan taken out to pay for real estate and that usually includes agreed upon interest rates and a payment schedule.

Note – a legal document that obligates a borrower to repay a loan at a specified interest

Pinnacle Score/Beacon Score - A number generated by the Equifax Credit Bureau to rank an individual's creditworthiness.

Prepayment – full or partial payment to the principal of a loan that is made before the designated due date

Prepayment Penalty – an amount charged for an early payoff of a loan

Promissory Note – a signed legal document that acknowledges the existence of a debt and the borrowers promise to repay it

Public Sale – a property auction that is open to the general public; a public sale generally requires notice (advertising) and must be held in a place accessible to the general public

Purchase – to obtain property in exchange for money

Tax Lien – a lien imposed on a property and/or person(s) for nonpayment of taxes

Tax Sale – public sale of a property at auction by a government authority as a result of nonpayment of taxes

Transunion – one of the three major credit bureaus.

Trustee – a person who is given legal responsibility, via a Deed of Trust or awarded by the court, to hold property in the best interest of or "for the benefit of" another

"I did then what I knew how to do. Now that I know better, I do better."

~Maya Angelo~

<u>Notes</u>

<u>Notes</u>

Notes

CREDIT SCORE

720-850

70‌719

675‌99

620‌674

560-619

500-559

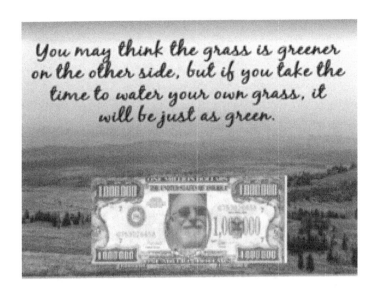

You may think the grass is greener on the other side, but if you take the time to water your own grass, it will be just as green.

More Books written by:
John Lee

Secrets of a Deal'ionaire

Creating Wealth One Small Deal at a Time

Foreword By *Robert Allen* – Multiple NY Times Best-selling author

"The reader cannot escape the conclusion the author knows his subject matter. I thought the government was the only one to make money out of taxes!" – William B. Beedie, Attorney

"In his new book, *Secrets of a Deal'ionaire*, John Lee teaches unique strategies for buying real estate with little or no money. *Secrets of a Deal'ionaire is* the 21st century's new book of *Nothing Down*." AJ Rassamni, author of Gain the Unfair Advantage

Other Books by:
John Lee

Secrets Those Credit Doctors Don't Want You to Know
&
Accompanying Workbook

The 1st Credit Book by: John Lee

How to Improve Your Credit Score

WHAT EVERYONE
NEEDS TO KNOW

John R Lee

The information contained in this text has come from experience, i.e. blood, sweat, tears, trials and errors. It started off as a necessity from my own circumstances, turned into a lifetime quest to help others. There's a lack of good information when it comes to your financial and credit well-being. My intent is to provide you with good information that you will be able to apply to your own situation. By opening these pages, you are taking a giant step towards upgrading your life. Regardless of where you are currently there is always room for improvement. Our goal is to share experiences that will be beneficial to you.

Another Groundbreaking Book by: John Lee

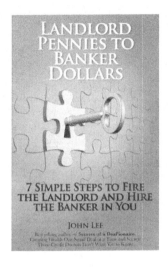

Landlord Pennies to Banker Dollars

Are you a landlord? Are you tired of the landlord myth of *Easy Passive Income*? Are you tired of *Toilets, Trash* and *Tenants?* Then this is for you.

With his revolutionary M.O.M. method, Lee shows you how to turn your hard-earned banker pennies into easy-collecting banker dollars.

A must read for all landlords and anyone who has ever thought of being a landlord.

About the Author John Lee the Deal'ionaire

John R Lee has been investing in unconventional, unique real estate deals for over 25 years. He was a mortgage broker for many years and also has an extensive insurance background.

Lee's been around the block more than once. John's also written several best-selling books including, "Secrets of a Deal'ionaire" , "Landlord Pennies to Banker Dollars" and "Secrets THOSE Credit Doctors Don't Want YOU to Know."

Today, Lee focuses on education and stresses how important it is for you to succeed. One of the most important things John has learned is to get a mentor and jump-start your way to success.

As he always says, "There are two ways to do things, the easy way or the hard way. A mentor will get you there the easy way. The hard way is to spend twenty-five years learning it by yourself. Investing is a team-sport."

John is most famous for showing you how to turn $200 into $2,000 with about 2 hours' worth of work. By doing so you can spend more time with your loved ones and doing things you want to do, like he does.

The secrets and strategies John share are unique and priceless. He has simplified processes that can be very complicated.

Secrets *THOSE* Credit Doctors Don't Want *YOU* to Know

7 Simple Steps to a Higher Credit Score
&
Avoiding a Debt Sentence

What Others are Saying…

Knowledge is Power

Everything you need about getting your credit where you want it to be is in this book! Must have. ~ Steve D. ~

A really good way to understand your credit

I did not have an expectation. I wanted to have an open mind. The info in this book, which includes the workbook, helps you understand your credit in a better way. ~ David W. ~

Gift for my child

This is a gift for my daughter to help her understand how to best use credit to her advantage.
~ Regina O. ~

Knowledge that will last you a lifetime

Excellent book. ~Charles B.~

Very glad this book is available

I have been looking for information regarding ways to improve my credit score. Many thanks.
~ Milton T. ~

To find out more about:

John Lee **and the Deal'ionaire's latest books and upcoming events, visit**

www.theDEALIONAIRE.com

You may also email John directly at

theDEALIONAIRE@gmail.com

Made in the USA
Columbia, SC
21 January 2020